AUTONOMY, AUTHORITY AND MORAL RESPONSIBILITY

Law and Philosophy Library

VOLUME 33

Managing Editors

FRANCISCO J. LAPORTA, *Department of Law,*
Autonomous University of Madrid, Spain

ALEKSANDER PECZENIK, *Department of Law, University of Lund, Sweden*

FREDERICK SCHAUER, *John F. Kennedy School of Government,*
Harvard University, Cambridge, Mass., U.S.A.

Former Managing Editors
AULIS AARNIO, MICHAEL D. BAYLES[†], CONRAD D. JOHNSON[†], ALAN MABE

Editorial Advisory Board

AULIS AARNIO, *Research Institute for Social Sciences,*
University of Tampere, Finland
ZENON BANKOWSKY, *Centre for Criminology and the Social and Philosophical*
Study of Law, University of Edinburgh
PAOLO COMANDUCCI, *University of Genua, Italy*
ERNESTO GARZÓN VALDÉS, *Institut für Politikwissenschaft,*
Johannes Gutenberg Universität Mainz
JOHN KLEINIG, *Department of Law, Police Science and Criminal*
Justice Administration, John Jay College of Criminal Justice,
City University of New York
NEIL MacCORMICK, *Centre for Criminology and the Social and*
Philosophical Study of Law, Faculty of Law, University of Edinburgh
WOJCIECH SADURSKI, *Faculty of Law, University of Sydney*
ROBERT S. SUMMERS, *School of Law, Cornell University*
CARL WELLMAN, *Department of Philosophy, Washington University*

The titles published in this series are listed at the end of this volume.

THOMAS MAY

*Clinical Ethics Center,
Memorial Medical Center
and
Department of Medical Humanities,
Southern Illinois University,
School of Medicine,
Springfield, Illinois, U.S.A.*

AUTONOMY, AUTHORITY AND MORAL RESPONSIBILITY

KLUWER ACADEMIC PUBLISHERS
DORDRECHT / BOSTON / LONDON

A C.I.P. Catalogue record for this book is available from the Library of Congress.

B
808.67
.M38
1998

ISBN 0-7923-4851-6

Published by Kluwer Academic Publishers,
P.O. Box 17, 3300 AA Dordrecht, The Netherlands.

Sold and distributed in the U.S.A. and Canada
by Kluwer Academic Publishers,
101 Philip Drive, Norwell, MA 02061, U.S.A.

In all other countries, sold and distributed
by Kluwer Academic Publishers,
P.O. Box 322, 3300 AH Dordrecht, The Netherlands.

Printed on acid-free paper

All Rights Reserved
©1998 Kluwer Academic Publishers
No part of the material protected by this copyright notice may be reproduced or
utilized in any form or by any means, electronic or mechanical,
including photocopying, recording or by any information storage and
retrieval system, without written permission from the copyright owner

Printed in the Netherlands.

ACKNOWLEDGMENTS

This project evolved over a number of years. It began while studying philosophy at Bowling Green State University, and continued through a year at the University of Minnesota, to my present position as Director of the Clinical Ethics Center, Memorial Medical Center and Southern Illinois University, School of Medicine.

I owe thanks to a number of people who read and discussed portions of this work at various stages. These include Antony Flew, John Gray, Jospeh Raz, Michael Bradie, Paul Tudico, and Jim Spence. Special thanks are due to Mark Aulisio, James Child, Christopher Morris and Loren Lomasky for reading through several drafts.

My greatest debt of gratitude, however, must go to two people who helped see the project through both intellectually and emotionally. The first is Jana Craig, who tolerated a constant mess as research gathered and drafts were discarded. Without Jana's emotional support, this book could not have been completed. The second, and by far the largest debt of gratitude, must go out to Ray Frey, who as my Ph.D. supervisor saw the early stages of the work through the revisions done long after I left Bowling Green. More than this, however, Ray taught me to do philosophy, never pushing my ideas in any direction but allowing me to develop a position which at times he disagrees with. In this, Ray taught me to judge the merit of philosophical work through the strength of the arguments, rather than the conclusion reached.

I would also like to acknowledge the following journals, where some of the material in this book has appeared:

1.) A version of Chapter Three appeared under the title "The Concept of Autonomy", <u>American Philosophical Quarterly</u>, vol.31, no.2 (April, 1994).

2.) Portions of Chapter Seven appeared under the title "On Raz and the Obligation to Obey the Law", <u>Law and Philosophy</u>, vol.16 (January, 1997).

TABLE OF CONTENTS

INTRODUCTION 1

PART ONE: AUTONOMY 9

CHAPTER ONE: THE IMPORTANCE OF AUTONOMY 11
    Autonomy as a Presupposition of Rules 17
    The Presupposition of Self-Control in the Law 20
    The Relationship Between Autonomy and Rules 23
    Self-Control and Threats to Responsibility 25

CHAPTER TWO: THE CONCEPT OF AUTONOMY 33
    Autonomy as Autarkeia 38
    Autarkeia in Aristotle 38
    Autarkeia in Kant 40
    The Inadequacy of Autarkeia for Practical Autonomy 47
    Autonomy as Self-Rule 48

CHAPTER THREE: DEVELOPING THE HELMSMAN METAPHOR 55
    Identifying Helmsmanship 62
    Compulsion 64
    Coercion 66
    The Sensible Man 68
    An Adequate Range of Options 71
    Conclusion 72

CHAPTER FOUR: ADDRESSING KANT'S CONCERNS 75
    Desires and Motivation 78
    Freedom of Will vs. Freedom of Action 80
    Motivation vs. Causation 83
    Akrasia 85
    Summary of "Part One: Autonomy" 94

PART TWO: AUTHORITY 97
Introduction to Part Two 99

CHAPTER FIVE: AUTONOMY AND NORMATIVE OBLIGATION 107
Practical Reason and Obligation 113
The Concept of Second-Order Reasons 115
A Second Concept of Second-Order Reasons 117
The Importance of the Distinction 119
Normative Principles 121

CHAPTER SIX: AUTHORITY AND OBLIGATION 125
I. The Nature of Authority 127
   Varieties of Authoritative Directives 130
   The Simple Requirement of Action 130
   Sophisticated Directives 133
   Conditional Directives 133
   The Exclusion of Behavior Theory 134
II. Reconciling Autonomy and Authority 136
   Voluntary Slavery 137
   The Dependence Thesis 139
   The Dependence Thesis Revised 141
   The Limits of Authority 144

CHAPTER SEVEN: AUTONOMY AND THE AUTHORITY OF LAW 149
On the Obligation to Obey the Law 155
Arguments Against An Obligation to Obey the Law 158
The Debate in Context 163
A Two-Level Model of the Obligation to Obey the Law 165
The Revised Dependence Thesis and the Law 168
Toward a Prima Facie Obligation to Obey the Law 171

BIBLIOGRAPHY 175

INTRODUCTION

INTRODUCTION

Questions about the relationship between autonomy and authority are raised in nearly every area of moral philosophy. Although the most obvious of these is political philosophy (especially the philosophy of law), the issues surrounding this relationship are by no means confined to this area. Indeed, as we shall see as this work progresses, the issues raised are central to moral psychology, religion, professional ethics, medical ethics, and the nature of moral systems generally.

Although the title of this work is <u>Autonomy, Authority and Moral Responsibility,</u> we shall be concerned with the more general question about the relationship between autonomy (or self-direction) and external influences, which I take to be any guide to behavior whose presence, content or substance is dependent upon something beyond the control of the agent. Something is beyond the control of the agent if the agent cannot determine whether or not it is present, what its content consists of, or whether or not (or in what way) it influences her. These "external" influences may include (but are not necessarily limited to) religious convictions (which guide behavior according to a doctrine whose content is established independently of the agent); moral obligations (which require action in accordance with some moral theory); and desires for objects or states of affairs whose presence (or absence) is beyond the control of the agent. Of course, external influences may also include the requirements of authority or law.

Let us consider a few examples, beginning with moral psychology. External considerations threaten to make the value of action dependent upon the presence or absence of certain conditions or states which are beyond the control of the agent. If external considerations are allowed to influence moral motivation, it appears it is the contingent presence of the external considerations which guide action. For example, take the pleasure principle. If I value pleasure and determine action according to what will result in the greatest amount of pleasure, it seems it is the amount of pleasure that will result from various potential actions, a set of facts which are beyond my control, which guides my determination of action. How can the agent's autonomy be compatible with the influence of these external considerations?

Another example of this question arises in a discussion concerning the nature of moral judgements by R.M. Hare.[1] Hare maintains that one of the fundamental characteristics about the way in which we understand moral judgements is that they are taken to be more than mere expressions of opinion. We believe that it matters what answer we give to moral questions, and that there are right and wrong answers. The answers to moral questions are constrained by formal requirements such as universalizability and prescriptivity,[2] which are independent of the agent's subjective opinions and tastes. This feature of morality is set as an apparent paradox by Hare against the notion that a person must answer moral questions for herself. If morality is to be constrained by formal requirements which are independent of the agent, how can the agent be said to be answering the moral question for herself?

Hare's apparent paradox is brought to light in the context of a discussion about the nature of moral judgements generally. But the problem is also present in the context of substantive moral theory. Let us take an example from theology. If an agent's moral commitment to Christianity leads the agent to determine the answer to moral questions by reference to the doctrines of the Christian religion, how can she be said to be answering the moral question for herself? The doctrines of the Christian religion are beyond the control of the agent.

In professional ethics, one's behavior is affected by the requirements of professional codes of conduct, and the hierarchical structure many professions exhibit. The nurse, for example, is under certain obligations to implement the orders prescribed by a physician in virtue of her professional role.[3] Are the requirements and obligations imposed by one's profession compatible with autonomy, or need one surrender one's autonomy when acting as a professional?

Finally, in medical ethics autonomy has assumed a very prominent role in delineating the rights of patients. Informed consent, for example, is built upon a notion of patient autonomy. But is this notion viable in the setting of the medical center? A patient is affected by a variety of influences in this setting. The advice of the physician is but one. The resources of the patient, and of the medical center, are two others. Is the notion of patient autonomy an illusion in the setting of the medical center, or can autonomy be understood in such a way that it can merit the prominent role it now assumes in medical ethics, despite these external influences?

INTRODUCTION 5

All of the above examples of the conflict between autonomy and external influences exhibit the same theoretical problem that is more obvious in the conflict between autonomy and political authority. Certain facts are present (for example, the fact that a certain action will result in a certain amount of pleasure; the fact that a judgement meets certain formal constraints so as to qualify as a moral judgement; the fact that Christian doctrine requires or prohibits X; the fact that one's profession requires Y; or the fact that the physician advises the patient to do Z). The presence of these facts influences the one's determination of action, just as the fact that an authority directs X or the law requires Y influences the subject's action. These facts are beyond the agent's control, and this feature seems to pose a threat to the agent's autonomy.

In this book, I will be examining in detail the threat which each of these external influences poses to autonomy. In chapter one ("The Importance of Autonomy") I examine why it is important to establish an adequate conception of autonomy through the need for a conception of autonomy to serve as a basis for moral responsibility. I also set up the problem to be resolved in the dissertation; namely, in what ways the notion of autonomy can be maintained in the face of external influences. The answer to this question will offer a model for understanding moral responsibility in the context of such influences as compulsive desires, akrasia, moral or religious convictions, hierarchical relationships, obligations to authority, and the obligation to obey the law.

In chapter two ("The Concept of Autonomy"[4]) I examine the roots of the concept of autonomy. The concept developed since Kant's writings has been built upon a concept of autarkeia, or self-sufficiency. I show how this concept fails to provide a basis for a useful concept of moral responsibility in a world where external influences affect nearly every decision an agent makes. I then develop a conception of autonomy based upon Aristotle's conception of rulers (autonomy here being self-rule of one's behavior), in which the metaphor of the "helmsman" (developed by Aristotle) offers a model of autonomy as steering one's own behavior in the context of external considerations.

The metaphor of the helmsman offers a model of autonomy which allows external considerations to influence an agent's determination of action, so long as these influences do not threaten the agent's ability to steer his own course (to paraphrase Aristotle, "as if carried away by wind or a storm"). Chapter three ("Developing the Helmsman Metaphor") examines when external influences might be considered compulsive, or coercive. The standard for determining this is a form of "sensible man" standard which is developed in Aristotle within the context of the helmsman metaphor. We consider an action to be compelled or coerced when **no** "sensible man" could have done otherwise. The helmsman metaphor can thus be used to understand when compulsion or coercion should be recognized as undermining an agent's self-control, and thus relieve the agent of moral responsibility for her behavior.

Chapter four ("Addressing Kant's Concerns") takes up the question of motivation and self-control. Do phenomena such as desire "cause" action in such a way that an agent's practical reason is slave to present desires? Should akrasia be recognized as a valid excuse for behavior? I argue that although desires motivate, this motivation does not undermine an agent's self-control. Although desires play a role in motivation, the agent retains control over whether a desire is effective in motivating action. I offer several arguments to show that human motivation cannot be adequately modelled without positing a strong role for the agent's evaluative faculty (for example, an agent's evaluative faculty is needed to assess "strength of desire"). I then examine the phenomenon of akrasia, and argue that traditional conceptions of weakness of will do not show that the agent has "lost control". The conclusion is that desires are considerations an agent steers action in light of, not determining causes of action. This model of motivation supports the model of autonomy developed through the "helmsman" metaphor in the previous chapters.

Chapter five ("Autonomy and Normative Obligation") examines the influence of normative obligation on the determination of action. Can I be obligated to act in a specific manner and retain a sense of autonomy? I argue that the answer to this question depends upon how the obligation affects the agent's practical reasoning. Using a model of second-order reasoning developed by Joseph Raz,[5] I distinguish two different ways that a second-order reason may operate within practical reason (a distinction which has been overlooked by Raz). One of these ways is compatible with autonomy, and the other is not.

INTRODUCTION

Chapter six ("Authority and Obligation") looks at how the obligation to obey authority might be made compatible with autonomy, and thus how we might view an agent as morally responsible for her actions even when acting under the orders of an authority. I first reject any attempts to make autonomy and authority compatible through the type of directives issued. I do this by showing how different varieties of authoritative directives are subject to the same basic problem of apparent incompatibility with autonomy. To make autonomy and authority compatible, the obligation to obey must be of the type described in the previous chapter as compatible with autonomy. I then examine the limits this imposes on authority, by making corrections to the "dependence thesis" (developed by Joseph Raz[6]) which not only allow the 'obligation to obey' to be of the type which is compatible with autonomy, but is more consistent with the model of authority offered by Raz himself.

In light of the model of authority developed in chapter six, in chapter seven ("Autonomy and the Authority of Law") I examine the authority of law, and how the requirements of law might be compatible with autonomy. This is an important issue if, for example, we wish to hold the Nazi judges responsible for sending Jews to death camps as prescribed under Nazi law. I begin by examining the nature of the obligation to obey the law. I first examine Joseph Raz's argument that the obligation to obey the law cannot be *prima facie*,[7] and show how this view results from his model of authority. Continuing with my refinements of Raz's model of authority, I show how the changes made to the "dependence thesis" in the previous chapter can allow us to understand the obligation to obey the law as *prima facie*, without threatening the content-independent character of law. This requires a two-level model of the obligation to obey the law based upon the model of authority developed in the previous chapter.

---

[1] Hare, R.M. Freedom and Reason, (New York: Oxford University Press, 1963).

[2] I do not wish to go into the details of Hare's theory here. We shall take this up in chapter five. For more on these formal requirements, see Hare, R.M. Freedom and Reason.

[3] I have written on this issue in an article titled "the Nurse Under Physician Authority" <u>Journal of Medical Ethics</u> (December 1993).

[4] I discussed the ideas which underlay this chapter in an article titled "The Concept of Autonomy", <u>American Philosophical Quarterly</u> (forthcoming).

[5] Raz, Joseph <u>Practical Reason and Norms,</u> (Princeton: Princeton University Press, 1990).

[6] Raz, Joseph <u>The Morality of Freedom,</u> New York: Oxford University Press, 1986).

[7] Raz, Joseph <u>The Authority of Law</u> (New York: Oxford University Press, 1979).

**PART ONE:
AUTONOMY**

CHAPTER ONE:
The Importance of Autonomy

THE IMPORTANCE OF AUTONOMY

The concept of autonomy has come to assume a place of great importance in recent discussions of practical and applied ethics. Since the writings of Immanuel Kant, autonomy has become nearly synonymous with human dignity, and an imminent value in any system which purports to place proper emphasis on the respect for persons as such. Thus, autonomy has assumed a prominent role in many areas of practical ethics: In medical ethics through informed consent;[1] in business ethics through advertising;[2] in constitutional law through privacy[3] and free speech;[4] and in social policy through establishing minimal standards of welfare[5] and debates on Paternalism.[6] Autonomy has even played a key role in the debate over animal rights.[7]

Autonomy has assumed this prominent role because it is a concept upon which we structure the world around us. As a characteristic of persons, autonomy is a fundamental concept for our perception of the world and our place in it. The way we perceive of ourselves as distinct from inanimate objects, the way in which we interact with our surroundings, and the way in which we understand the causes and responsibility for the events which take place around us are wrapped up in our conception of autonomy. In this way, autonomy is a vital concept for the way in which we understand our world.

Even our common understanding of our identity itself focuses upon autonomous action.[8] There is a common identification of actions to persons only when the person in question exercises a certain control over action. For example, when we are coerced to perform a certain action, it is quite common to excuse ourselves by saying, "that wasn't me...". Likewise, when under the influence of a drug (such as alcohol, for example) which threatens our control over our actions, we are quick to say "That was the alcohol speaking, not me..." and provide other similar excuses based upon the lack of identification of behavior to the person in question.

This connection between autonomy and identity is often misunderstood. For example, the theory of autonomy advanced by Gerald Dworkin[9] attempts to understand autonomy in terms of identity, which is opposite of the understanding I offer. Dworkin's view of autonomy is that autonomous behavior is behavior we "identify" with, recognizing that we wish at some deep level to be the type of person who acts in this way. Dworkin describes this as follows:

> It is the attitude a person takes toward the influences motivating him which determines whether or not they are to be considered "his". Does he identify with them, assimilate them to himself, view himself, as the kind of person who wishes to be motivated in these particular ways? If, on the contrary, a man resents his being motivated in certain ways, is alienated from those influences, resents acting in accordance with them, would prefer to be the kind of person who is motivated in different ways, then those influences, even though they may be causally effective, are not viewed as "his".[10]

For Dworkin, autonomous behavior is precisely that behavior which we identify with. But it seems that Dworkin has the relationship between autonomy and identification reversed. It is not that autonomous behavior is that behavior we identify with, it is that those behaviors we identify with are autonomous behaviors.

Consider our reaction to behavior which is required. The fact that it is required seems to detract from its appropriateness for praise, and many even feel that the fact that it is required robs them of the ability to feel it is they who choose to do this (even though they recognize that if it weren't required, they would like to be the sort of person who acts in the manner which is currently required). Charity is a good example of this. When charity is required, it seems to detract from the praiseworthiness of charitable acts, even if we still feel charity is a good thing.

For Dworkin, autonomy requires a certain attitude toward the influences motivating a person, and does not require that the person *actually determine her behavior*. For Dworkin, certain paternalistic laws might be compatible with autonomy if the subject recognizes that she would like to be the sort of person who acts in the way that the law requires. This is true even though it is clear that the determination of behavior is done by the law in question. All Dworkin requires is that the attitude we take toward this "external" determination of action be one of "identification" as described above. This is simply not how we understand and apply the concept of autonomy in any ordinary sense.

We **identify** with our behavior when we feel *we have chosen it*, and to require behavior detracts from our identification with it, even if we wish to be the sort of person who acts in that way. It is not the "attitude the actor takes toward the influences motivating him" which lead him to identify with behavior (as Dworkin argues), but the recognition that *the agent herself determines the action* which leads the agent to identify with the action.[11]

Because our identity is so closely linked to autonomy, and because it is in terms of autonomous individuals that we organize our perception of the world and the place of persons in it, we wish to take steps to preserve autonomy as a characteristic of persons. To undercut this characteristic is to require a complete reconceptualization of our understanding of how we identify values, account for why certain things happen, and justify our relationships with others. Thus, we are concerned to recognize the right to informed consent. We are concerned to place limitations on servitude (for example, we cannot sell ourselves into slavery). Indeed, the Bill of Rights attached to the U.S. Constitution is a tangible indication of the significance which is attached to the recognition of autonomy in American society.[12] Autonomy is central to our understanding of ourselves, and thus we wish to protect this characteristic of persons.

Perhaps nowhere is the notion of autonomy more crucial as a basis of our understanding of the world and our place in it than in society. Because we identify with our autonomous actions, autonomy becomes a crucial concept for understanding the notion of moral responsibility which underpins the various ways in which society operates. The ways in which we interact with others and the variety of ways in which we regulate this behavior (such as cultural norms, religious convictions, hierarchical structures and legal systems just to name a few) require an understanding of behavior in terms of autonomous individuals. As we shall see below, autonomy is vital for regulating behavior through rules.

It is this role which makes autonomy the prominent "super value" that it is. It is a value which we do not trade off with other values in normal ways. For example, we do not allow autonomy to be traded for goods, or sold (by selling oneself into slavery). It is a value which seems to enjoy special precedence over other values. For example, in medical ethics autonomy is often held to be more important even than the curing of an illness when we allow persons the right to refuse treatment.

Why do we view autonomy so differently than other values? There is nothing "super valuable" about autonomy per se. Indeed, we find many instances of people who hold autonomy to be less valuable than other goals and aspirations,[13] and whole systems of justice which deny that the value of autonomy is more important than welfare.[14] To understand the role autonomy has assumed as a "super value", we must recognize that it is not that autonomy per se is what we take to be a "super value", it is that autonomy is such a vital concept for our organization of the world and our place in it which confers upon autonomy the status of "super value".

What makes autonomy a "super value" is the role it plays in our understanding of the world, and the fundamental role it thus plays in the way we structure and organize society. In this, autonomy is a *societal* value. Because autonomy is important for the ways we organize our world and thus for the ways we organize society, its value in this role *supersedes* the value any particular individual places upon it. This is why we do not easily allow people to trade their autonomy off; it undercuts the way in which we structure society. Indeed, this is why we are concerned to protect autonomy as a characteristic of persons. To the extent that we can recognize persons as autonomous, we are better able to understand their role in society and organize society appropriately. When the autonomy of persons is called into question, it poses great difficulty for our understanding of their place in society and how we may appropriately view (and regulate) their behavior. Examples of this can be seen with soldiers at *My Lai*, Nazi war criminals, the insane, and persons acting under various obligations. These situations pose great difficulties.

It is in light of this role as a fundamental concept for our understanding of the world and our organization of society that I shall be concerned to develop a concept of autonomy. In particular, I shall be concerned to develop a concept of autonomy which can serve as a basis of moral responsibility. In this, I shall be concerned to develop a *practical* concept of autonomy, a concept we can use to distinguish those behaviors we can be said to control the direction of from those behaviors we cannot. A practical concept of autonomy is vital to clarify the issues autonomy has come to assume a prominent role within, and to develop models of social organization which both protect this characteristic of persons, and regulate behavior in a feasible manner.

First, though, let us look more closely at the fundamental role autonomy plays in our understanding of the world, and how this serves as a basis for the ways in which we organize society. We shall do this by examining the fundamental role which a concept of autonomy must play in any society which attempts to regulate behavior through rules.

Autonomy as a Presupposition of Rules

The unique feature of rules is that they regulate conduct in a particular way: by specifying the required behavior, and expecting the subject to then conform his behavior to this requirement.[15] In this, rules require a positive effort to comply which cannot be achieved passively. Simple coincidence of actual and required behavior is not rule-following.

In this, engaging in the behavior which constitutes conforming to the rule requires specific effort of a sort not required when acting upon one's natural inclinations, as H.L.A. Hart observes:

> ...But where the law runs counter to strong inclinations as, for example, do laws requiring the payment of taxes, our eventual compliance with them, even though regular, has not the unreflective, effortless, engrained character of habit.[16]

The specific behavior which constitutes conformity to rules is not "natural", even though obedience in the abstract may in some cases be. Indeed, rules are often required to supersede an agent's own immediate inclinations, and indeed it is this feature of rules which leads to the sus picion that rules threaten autonomy.[17] Because the behavior required is not "natural", one must be presumed to have control over the direction of one's behavior in order to direct behavior away from "natural tendencies" or habits and to a specific (required) behavior if one is to be able to conform one's behavior to the rule.

The unnaturalness of the conformity to rules also explains why it is often necessary to enforce rules in some way in order to ensure conformity. For this reason, we often attach rewards or sanctions of some sort to the conformity or lack of conformity of behavior to various rules. In fact, for H.L.A. Hart the appropriateness of such reward and sanction of behavior distinguishes rule-following from habit:

> First, for the group to have a habit it is enough that their behaviour in fact converges. Deviation from the regular course need not be a matter for any form of criticism. But such general convergence or even identity of behavior is not enough to constitute the existence of a rule requiring that behaviour: where there is such a rule deviations are generally regarded as lapses or faults open to criticism, and threatened deviations meet with pressure for conformity, though the forms of criticism and pressure differ with different types of rules.[18]

Hart goes even further in stating that the existence of the rule in some sense *justifies* criticism of deviation, and pressure to conform.[19] The important point here, however, is that the social pressure described by Hart above is often necessary because the behavior required is not natural.

To act contrary to one's inclinations requires one to have control over the direction of her behavior. To the extent that social pressure and criticism is necessary to secure conformity, autonomy must again be presupposed because social pressure would be futile were the agent simply unable to conform her behavior to the rule (and a lack of control over behavior would entail such an inability). Thus, criticism of deviations or incentives to conform require one to have control over her behavior. In the words of Thomas Nagel, "It seems irrational to take or dispense credit or blame for matters over which a person has no control."[20] It is this control over behavior, then, which we build a concept of moral responsibility upon.

Nagel's statement concerning the ascription of praise and blame reflects a fundamental intuitive presumption which most people seem to share about the notion of moral responsibility: the concept of moral responsibility only applies when the person "could have done otherwise." This presupposition has been held by a wide diversity of thinkers, from classical thinkers such as Aristotle[21] and Augustine[22] to modern day thinkers such as Peter Strawson.[23] Perhaps more important than these historical roots, however, is the intuitive appeal which this view seems to have with the great majority of people,[24] and its wide application in our everyday lives.[25] It is the agent's control over behavior which allows us to assign responsibility for the behavior to the agent in question.

Consider an appeal to intuitions offered by John Martin Fischer. Fischer asks us to imagine that we discover that the behavior of a friend is being electronically manipulated by a team of scientists. These scientists have secretly implanted a device in our friend's brain which allows them to monitor the activities of his brain. Whenever our friend deliberates, the device is used to stimulate the brain to induce certain decisions. Fischer concludes that upon discovery of the manipulation of our friend by the scientists, a fundamental change would take place in our attitude toward his behavior:

> At first it would be hard to know how one would react to such an unusual situation. But, I think, once you had been convinced that direct manipulation exists, a striking thing would occur: many of your most basic *attitudes* toward your friend would change. Your friend would no longer seem to be an appropriate object of such attitudes as respect, gratitude, love, indignation, and resentment. Furthermore, it would somehow seem out of place to praise or blame your friend on the basis of his behavior.[26]

Fischer's example may seem to some to be far-fetched, or a problem only in science fiction novels. However, variations of this change in attitude are apparent almost everywhere one looks. For example, we do not hold the insane responsible for crimes, as we believe them to lack control in some fundamental sense. We do not hold children responsible to the extent we do adults. We do not hold people responsible for behavior which is compelled, coerced, or performed out of necessity.

Without the ability to ascribe moral responsibility to an agent for her conformity (or lack thereof) to a rule, we lose the ability to identify the deviant agent and bring the appropriate pressure to bear upon her. Any social pressure designed to secure conformity to a rule must be brought to bear upon an agent within whose power it is to secure conformity.

The Presupposition of Self-Control in the Law

The clearest examples of the presupposition of self-control for rule-governed behavior lies in the law. For example, Jeremy Bentham maintains that the conditions of responsibility (e.g. that the action be voluntary, the agent have minimal mental capacities, etc.) are simply the conditions required for the threat of punishment to be effective in securing conformity.[27]

This presupposition of self-control can also be seen in limitations upon the types of effective laws one can make. Lon Fuller offers eight ways in which one can fail to make law.[28] These are as follows: (1) The failure to make rules generalized, so that decisions are made on an ad-hoc basis; (2) The failure to adequately publicize the rules; (3) Making rules which are retroactive in nature; (4) The Failure to make rules understandable; (5) Making rules which are contradictory; (6) Making rules which require conduct beyond the power of the subject; (7) Making excessively frequent changes in the rules; (8) A failure of congruence between the rules as announced and their actual administration.[29]

In particular, (3) through (6) above embody directly the importance of self-control in regulating behavior through law. While (1), (2), (7) and (8) are also related to the presupposition of self-control (For example, the failure to adequately publicize the rules undermines self-control through the need for information in order to act upon the rules), they are related to self-control in *Fuller's* work only indirectly. Because Fuller discusses the defect of these failures in terms which are not *directly* tied to self-control, we shall not discuss them in depth here. I shall focus on those failures to make law which are directly rooted in self-control. After all, as Fuller states, "A total failure in any one of these eight directions does not simply result in a bad system of law; it results in something that is not properly called a legal system at all...".[30]

Retroactive rules cannot govern behavior because, since they are made after-the-fact, it is impossible to direct conduct in the present according to such rules. By directing behavior after-the-fact, the rule circumvents the subject's ability to conform her behavior to the rule. Similarly, the failure to make rules understandable undermines the subject's ability to conform behavior to the rule, for as Fuller asks, "How can anybody follow a rule that nobody can understand?".[31] The defect in each case is the absence of an ability to conform behavior to the rule because the subject does not know what behavior is required by the rule when the subject is determining behavior.

Contradictory rules, Fuller tells us, fail to give meaningful direction. By requiring contradictory action, one must not conform to some rule in order to conform to some other rule. Thus, one is never able to conform one's behavior to the requirements of the system of rules as a whole, and is therefore always subject to punishment. States Fuller:

> A man who is habitually punished for doing what he was ordered to do can hardly be expected to respond appropriately to orders given him in the future. If our treatment of him is part of an attempt to build up a system of rules for the governance of his conduct, then we shall fail in that attempt.[32]

I will go even further than Fuller on this point. It is not simply that we will be ineffective in governing the subject's conduct by passing contradictory laws, it is that we fail to direct his conduct at all. By requiring 'X' and 'not X', we provide no direction, and we undermine the subject's ability to conform her behavior to the system of rules.

Clearly in all three of the cases considered thus far, the agent's ability to conform her behavior to the rule is of paramount importance. In order for a rule to govern the behavior of a subject, the subject must also have control over the determination of her behavior, otherwise she lacks the ability to conform her behavior to the rule.

The importance of the ability to conform one's behavior to the rule is most obvious when Fuller discusses rules which require the impossible. If rules are to govern the subject's behavior, the behavior required must be within the power of the subject; otherwise, it is impossible that the rule should govern the subject's behavior.

I do not wish here, to maintain that all forms of social and legal liability are based upon a concept of autonomy. Nor do I wish to argue that all forms of social and legal liability *should* be based upon a concept of autonomy. I simply wish to show that the vast majority of contexts in which the question of responsibility arises are underpinned by an understanding of behavior in terms of autonomous individuals. This is because we understand our own identity and our relationship to the world in these terms. But there may be contexts in which we feel another concept of responsibility better serves the purposes of society, and in these cases we need not employ a concept of responsibility which presupposes autonomy.

The best example of such a phenomenon is the idea of strict liability.[33] But strict liability is generally concerned with distributing costs effectively, rather than regulating behavior. In this, the concept of responsibility sought is one of *causal* responsibility only, with no concern for *moral* responsibility. It is precisely because of the lack of identification of the agent to the behavior in some fundamental moral sense that such offenses rarely contain the moral stigma which is attached to issues of moral responsibility. In those cases in which this is not true, such as statutory rape, we simply feel the violation of the rule is so repugnant that we wish to punish the behavior whether or not it was within the control of the agent. But notice just how rare these cases are. Normally, we are very uncomfortable with any organization of society which is not based upon an understanding of behavior in terms of autonomy. So much so, in fact, that even many cases of strict liability contain residual elements of a presumption of control. For the sake of brevity and focus, I refer the reader to L.H. Leigh, <u>Strict and Vicarious Liability</u>, for a discussion of the presumption of control in strict liability, complete with examples.[34]

The Relationship Between Autonomy and Rules

I should say something about the relationship between rules and autonomy in order to avoid confusion later. In the later chapters of this work I shall be concerned with the compatibility of rules and autonomy, asking when they are compatible and when they are not. In this chapter, I am examining the presupposition of autonomy which must be made if a system of rules is to be effective. These are not the same question.

I have argued above that autonomy must serve as a basis of moral responsibility, and through this be presupposed by an effective system of rules. This does not, however, mean that the rules themselves do not threaten autonomy. Indeed, rules in various forms are one of the most common threats to autonomy posited by writers on the subject.[35] This is because rules direct behavior in a way which seems to pre-empt the subject's direction of her own behavior. If the subject's direction of behavior is in fact pre-empted, it seems inappropriate to hold her responsible for behavior performed under the direction of the rules. It is this problem which faced the World War Two Allies when trying many Nazi war criminals, particularly Nazi judges who argued that they were required to implement the rules of the legal system regardless of their own beliefs.[36] Let us examine this in greater detail.

It seems inappropriate to hold a person responsible for behavior directed by rules because the subject in some sense seems to be unable to bring her behavior in line with what is expected, and at the same time recognize the requirements of the rules.[37] For example, it is often said that the Nazi judges should be held accountable to a "higher law", but the threat which the legal rules of Nazi Germany pose to the autonomy of the judges threatens to undermine this system of "higher laws", if we expect judges to implement the law as it is written rather than their own conscience. If the judges lack the ability to bring their behavior in line with "higher laws" because the ability to act on their own judgement is pre-empted by their obligation to implement the legal rules of Nazi Germany, this inability to bring their behavior in line with "higher laws" undermines the ability of the "higher laws" to regulate behavior.

However, while the presence of rules in the above examples might pose a threat to autonomy, the very rules which pose this threat must presuppose the autonomy of the subject if the rule is to regulate behavior. Thus, a judge who is not autonomous *cannot* bring his behavior in line with the requirements of the laws of Nazi Germany, just as these requirements then threaten his ability to conform to "higher laws". The phenomenon of coercion provides a good analogy to this discussion. Coercion presupposes the evaluative faculty of the subject of coercion, yet is a paradigm instance of a threat to the subject's self-control. The very nature of a coercive statement such as "I will kill you unless you do X", relies upon the subject's valuing life, yet the action which results is said to reflect the values of the person who coerces, not the subject of coercion.[38] Similarly, rules (and other external influences) might be held to coerce or compel behavior despite their reliance upon the subject's autonomy in securing conformity. This is especially true if we allow that a person's desires, values, commitments and obligations may at times "bind" the person to, for example, do that which she is committed to, or obligated to do.

Thus, we must distinguish the autonomy which is presupposed by a system of rules from whether the subject has or lacks autonomy under that system of rules. Rules cannot hope to effectively regulate the behavior of a non-autonomous subject. To conform behavior to rules, one must have control over the direction of one's behavior. Thus we must limit our attempts to regulate behavior through rules to agents who can be said to have control over the direction of their behavior, and circumstances in which the agent is able to exercise this control. It is an additional question, then, whether the subject retains autonomy under the rule. This question must ask whether the agent remained in control of the direction of her behavior, or if the rule directed behavior. We shall discuss the threat which rules pose to autonomy in the latter chapters of this work. Here, we are concerned with the presupposition of autonomy by rules.

Self-Control and Threats to Responsibility

To this point, I hope to have shown that a system of rules which hopes to *effectively* govern behavior must presuppose a notion of self-control to serve as a basis of moral responsibility. As we have seen, the recognition of what is within an agent's control, and thus what exactly may be required by a rule, is essential not only negatively in the sense that rules which circumvent the subject's self-control cannot govern her conduct, but also positively in that a recognition of what an agent is responsible for is necessary to secure actual conformity to the rule. Given the context of the way in which we understand our world and the relationship of people to it, in order for normative rules to effectively regulate behavior, the concept of autonomy *must* be recognized as a basis of moral responsibility.

Similarly, when judging rule-directed behavior itself by "higher laws" or other standards, it is necessary to ask whether the rules themselves threatened the autonomy of the subject, or allowed the subject to retain a measure of self-control necessary for the ascription of praise and blame. Although the presence of rules presupposes autonomous subjects, it does not follow that the subject remains autonomous under those rules. Likewise, the threat which any external influence poses to autonomy threatens to undermine the viability of regulating behavior through rules.

Exactly what self-control is and how it is effected by various influences remains unclear. Susan Wolf discusses this relationship between control and responsibility in her book <u>Freedom Within Reason</u>:

> Dogs and cats, young children, the insane, and severely mentally retarded adults have potentially effective wills, and yet we do not regard them as responsible beings. Though these individuals have a kind of control of their behavior, they cannot control their behavior along the right lines.[39]

What does it mean to "control behavior along the right lines"? Wolf gives us a clue as to the nature of such control when she tells us that it must be possible for the "features which weigh in favor of or against" an agent's performing a particular action to enter into the agent's determination of action.[40] On this account, it seems that an evaluational judgement (or assessment) on the part of the agent, a judgement which directs the agent's behavior, is crucial to the concepts of self-control and responsibility. It seems that the notion of responsibility requires that the agent play an active role in the determination of her behavior rather than simply reacting to "external" forces, by assessing the factors for and against various alternatives.

Throughout this work, we shall be concerned with autonomy as it is affected by a variety of external influences. In this, we shall be considering the autonomy of the subject within the system of influences: do the influences determine behavior, or does the subject retain a sense of self-control even when subject to these influences. This question is important, for just as the moral responsibility which was required for ascriptions of praise and blame made a presumption of self-control, to morally praise or blame behavior performed under various forms of influence, the behavior must reflect the subject's ability to control the direction of her behavior. Thus, we will be interested in the affect of various external influences upon the agent's autonomy.

Do external considerations threaten self-control by dictating action in accordance withparticular consequences? Do moral requirements threaten self-control by dictating action according to moral obligations? Does authority threaten self-control by subverting the agent's practical reasoning to the dictates of authority? All of the above have been considered threats to self-control, and thus moral responsibility, by some theorists.[41]

Real-world examples of these questions and the controversy which surrounds them are not difficult to find. Consider, for example, the intuitive tensions surrounding the outlook we take on the following cases: At the Nuremberg Trials after World War Two, a common defense offered by Nazi war criminals consisted of an appeal to the fact that they had no control: "I was only following orders." Compare this defense with a similar defense offered by soldiers at My Lai during the Vietnam War, or a nurse administering drugs prescribed by a physician (which result in some negative effects).[42] Are such behaviors immune to moral evaluation because they are performed under orders? If not, in what way can the subject be said to have control over the direction of her behavior when specific behavior is required by the authority?

Similarly, we can find a plethora of questions concerning responsibility and its compatibility with moral obligations. If the Church of Scientology prohibits the use of technological medical treatments, are parents responsible for withholding such treatment from their children if they do so because of a commitment to the teachings of the Church of Scientology? Is the person who allows a rape, murder or assault to take place (rather than use violence to prevent it) because of a commitment to pacifism responsible for his failure to prevent such harm? Is the religious zealot responsible for the persecution of heretics which is prescribed by the church?

Related to these questions, and to some extent presupposed by them, are metaphysical questions of self-control. It is also easy to find real-world examples of these questions. For example, can severely mentally retarded people, or the insane, be held responsible for their behavior? Is a hiker stranded in a blizzard and faced with death from starvation and cold responsible for her behavior if she breaks into a cabin to obtain food and shelter? Or should she be considered to in some sense have been compelled to act as she did by the circumstances she was in? If so, when should circumstances be said to compel behavior in this manner, and when should the hiker be said to be responsible for her action even though she was in difficult circumstances?

In fact, can we ever really be said to have control over the direction of our behavior, or are all of our behaviors determined by a natural lottery of natural and mental abilities, the arbitrary circumstances we are in, etc.? John Rawls, for example, maintains that we cannot claim responsibility for our native endowments, our starting place in society, or the "superior character" which enables a person to cultivate and develop his talents and native endowments. We possess these things through luck (a "natural lottery") and have no control over them.[43]

These questions are difficult, some would even say paradoxical, but they are questions that cannot be ignored. As Thomas Nagel observes concerning the problem of moral responsibility:

> ...The degree to which the problem has a solution can be determined only by seeing whether in some degree the incompatibility between this conception and the various ways in which we do not control what we do is only apparent.[44]

Part of the purpose of this work is to develop a concept of autonomy which may help to clarify the controversy surrounding the notion of moral responsibility. In particular, we shall concern ourselves with the fundamental question of whether an agent may regulate her behavior according to external influences and retain a viable sense of self-control? Authority and obligation may then be analyzed as types of external influences within this prior discussion.

Let us begin by examining the perspective autonomy takes toward external influences and the threat which these influences do and do not pose to autonomy. In the next chapter, I shall argue that we must reconceptualize autonomy, jettisoning the concept which has developed since the writings of Immanuel Kant. Kant's conception of autonomy was developed to understand moral value, and is too rigorous in the perspective it takes toward external influences. This rigor renders the Kantian conception of autonomy unable to serve as a basis of moral responsibility in a world in which external considerations influence our every decision.

In place of Kant's conception of autonomy, I will offer in the following chapters a model of autonomy which takes a perspective on external influences that allows their presence without necessarily threatening autonomy. It is this perspective on external influences which the concept of autonomy must take if it is to serve a useful role in our understanding of the world. What makes autonomy the value that it is tied to its role in organizing society. To serve in this role, the concept of autonomy must be compatible with the variety of external influences which are a part of our everyday lives, and affect nearly every decision we take. It must help us distinguish influences which threaten autonomy from influences which do not. It must recognize the roles of various forms of authority in our daily lives. If the concept of autonomy is not developed along these lines, it simply cannot serve in the prominent role which it now assumes in contemporary applied ethics.

[1] See Faden, Ruth and Beauchamp, Tom A History and Theory of Informed Consent (New York: Oxford University Press, 1986).
[2] See Haworth, Lawrence Autonomy (New Haven: Yale University Press, 1986).
[3] See Richards, David A.J. Sex, Drugs, Death and the Law (Rowman and Littlefield, 1982).
[4] See Scanlon, Thomas "A Theory of Freedom of Expression", Philosophy and Public Affairs 1, (Winter 1972).
[5] See Raz, Joseph The Morality of Freedom, (New York: Oxford University Press, 1986).
[6] See Sartorius, Rolf (ed.) Paternalism, (University of Minnesota Press, 1983).
[7] See Frey, R.G. "Autonomy and the Value of Animal Life", The Monist vol.70, no.1 (January 1987).
[8] Derek Parfit would deny that the separate identity of persons is how we should understand personal identity (see Parfit, Derek Reasons and Persons, New York: Oxford University Press, 1984). While there may be good philosophical reasons for believing that we should jettison individual identity in formulating a theoretical understanding of persons, I am concerned here with the role autonomy plays in our common understanding of personal identity. In this realm, autonomy is central to how we identify actions with specific persons.
[9] See Dworkin, Gerald "Autonomy and Behavior Control", The Hastings Center Report (Feb. 1976).
[10] Dworkin, Gerald "Autonomy and Behavior Control", p.25.
[11] Dworkin's position is based upon an attempt to understand autonomy in terms of free will. We shall take up the problems with this approach in later chapters.
[12] Because we take autonomy so seriously, our concern with its recognition identifies certain rights which we wish to have in order to protect this characteristic. Indeed, throughout this work we shall be examining how autonomy might be preserved in light of a variety of external influences.
[13] For example, monks believe that their autonomy is less important than serving the will of God. Others might hold that their autonomy is less important than security, for example, and so wish to trade off this characteristic for the security of

servitude. However, we place severe limitations on these trade offs, and these limitations reflect the special status autonomy has.

[14] For example, we often recognize a need to limit what damage people are able to do to their own welfare.

[15] I owe the foundations of this idea to James Child, who has written at length on the idea in a variety of unpublished papers which shall (hopefully) soon comprise a manuscript on the subject. These papers include "The Rule of Law and the Presumption of Autonomy"; "Specific Commands, General Rules and Degrees of Autonomy"; and "Wittgenstein, Davidson and Section 2.01 of the *Model Penal Code*".

[16] Hart, H.L.A. The Concept of Law, (New York: Oxford University Press, 1961), p.51.

[17] We shall take up the threat which rules pose to autonomy in later chapters. At this point, however, we are merely concerned to show that rules themselves presuppose autonomous subjects, even if the rule may then threaten the subject's autonomy.

[18] Hart, H.L.A. The Concept of Law, p.54.

[19] Hart, H.L.A. The Concept of Law, pp.54-55.

[20] Nagel, Thomas "Moral Luck", in Mortal Questions (New York: Cambridge University Press, 1979), p.28.

[21] Aristotle, Nicomachean Ethics bk.3, in The Basic Works of Aristotle ed. by Richard McKeon (New York: Random House, 1941).

[22] Augustine, On Free Will, bk.3, in Free Will ed. by Sidney Morgenbresser and James Walsh (New Jersey: Prentice-Hall, 1962).

[23] Strawson, P.F. "Freedom and Resentment" Proceedings of the British Academy 48, pp.1-25.

[24] This intuitive appeal is quite strong among philosophers as well. For a discussion of this intuitive appeal, see Frankfurt, Harry "Alternate Possibilities and Moral Responsibility", Journal of Philosophy LXVI, no.23 (December 4, 1969).

[25] Again, I am most concerned to show that this is in fact the way we understand responsibility in everyday usage, and that this reflects the way we understand the world and the place of agents within it. My goal here is to establish the claim I made at the beginning of this chapter: That the concept of autonomy is vital as a fundamental concept for the way in which we understand the world around us, and our place in this world.

[26] Fischer, John Martin (ed.) Moral Responsibility (Ithaca: Cornell University Press, 1986), p.9.

[27] Benthem, Jeremy Principles of Morals and Legislation, (Reprinted in Buffalo: Prometheus Books, 1988), chapter XIII.

[28] Fuller, Lon The Morality of Law, (New Haven: Yale University Press, 1964), pp. 33-94.

[29] These eight ways one can fail to make law can be found listed in Fuller, The Morality of Law, p.39.

[30] Fuller, The Morality of Law, p.39.

31Fuller, The Morality of Law, p.36.

32Fuller, The Morality of Law, p.66.

33See Coleman, Jules Markets, Morals and the Law (New York: Cambridge University Press, 1988), especially chapter seven, "The Morality of Strict Tort Liability".

[34]Leigh, L.H. Strict and Vicarious Liability (London: Sweet and Maxwell, 1982), especially chapter one.

[35]For example, see Wolff, Robert Paul In Defense of Anarchism (New York: Harper & Row, 1970).

[36]See Taylor, Telford Nuremberg and Vietnam: An American Tragedy (New York: Bantam Books, 1971).

[37]Let us accept, for the sake of establishing the possible threat, that the obligation to conform to a rule might pre-empt a subject's practical reason in such a way that she cannot recognize this obligation and also act other than the obligation requires. We shall take up this question in much greater detail in later chapters.

[38]We shall take up the discussion of coercion in detail in chapter three.

[39]Wolf, Susan Freedom Within Reason (New York: Oxford University Press, 1990), p.7.

[40]Wolf, Freedom Within Reason, p.8.

[41]For example, see Wolff, Robert Paul In Defense of Anarchism (New York: Harper & Row, 1970); Adams, Robert Merrihew The Virtue of Faith (New York: Oxford University Press, 1987); Young, Robert Personal Autonomy: Beyond Negative and Positive Liberty (New York: St. Martin's Press, 1986).

[42]I have discussed this particular issue concerning the responsibility of the nurse when acting under the orders of a physician in an article entitled "The Nurse Under Physician Authority" Journal of Medical Ethics (Dec. 1993).

[43]Rawls, John A Theory of Justice (Cambridge: Harvard University Press, 1971), p.104.

[44]Nagel, "Moral Luck", p.38.

CHAPTER TWO:
The Concept of Autonomy

Despite the rise in prominence of the concept of autonomy, the concept remains vague at best. Joel Feinberg attributes this vagueness to the fact that autonomy is used in different contexts,[1] although he admits the uses are closely related. Gerald Dworkin attributes the vagueness of the concept to the fact that 'autonomy' is a "term of art",[2] which will not repay an Austinian investigation into its uses. But the concept of autonomy is used in very concrete roles, and is a key issue in many practical debates. If the concept is to serve in this role, we must have an idea of just what the concept is about, if only in the abstract.

Particularly vague is the relationship between autonomy and various influences upon an agent. If the concept of autonomy is to serve a useful role in applied ethics, it must be compatible with various forms of authority and other external influences which are important parts of our daily lives. For example, we all recognize the need to appeal to outside "authority" in many facets of life. We cannot learn medicine, law, mechanical skills, etc., adequately enough to perform each at an acceptable level. Therefore, we need to appeal to different forms of authority in some of these areas.

In a practical social context, the regularity and stability provided by the authoritative rules of society seems necessary for any meaningful sense of self-determination.[3] Traffic laws, for example, allow me to efficiently move from place to place, and in this way enhance, rather than threaten, my ability to determine my own activities. In the words of Gray Lankford Dorsey,

> (The) necessity for cooperative action is the particular source of the necessity of authority to freedom, for in order to cooperate men must know what behavior will be expected of them and what behavior they may expect from others...For these expectations to be known and fulfilled, there must be rules which are commonly followed.[4]

Not only is such predictability required for cooperative actions, but also is vital for individual self-determination, as F.A. Hayek observes:

> The law tells (an individual) what facts he may count on

and thereby extends the range within which he can predict the consequences of his actions...The law thus serves to enable the individual to act effectively on his own knowledge.[5]

Positioned against this view of the compatibility of autonomy and authority are the Libertarians, who see authority as fundamentally incompatible with autonomy. Libertarians often link autonomy to negative freedom. In doing so, the legitimate function of authority is seen to be the removal of "artificial" (man-made) obstacles to man's self-determination. This Libertarian notion views self-determination in a way similar to what Isaiah Berlin defines as "negative liberty".[6] In Berlin's characterization, you lack this freedom only if you are prevented from attaining a goal by human beings. Mere incapacity to attain a goal does not constitute a lack of negative liberty. In this way, the incapacity to move efficiently from place to place which results from the absence of traffic law is not viewed as a limitation on autonomy by Libertarians, while the interference with my driving preferences imposed by a body of (man-made) traffic law is.

However, the absence of man-made obstacles involved in negative liberty seems inadequate for the robust conception of autonomy employed throughout applied ethics. There seem to be certain positive factors which must be present for autonomy to be recognized. Joseph Raz,[7] for example, believes that in addition to independence from coercion, autonomy requires that a person be able to understand how choices will affect her life, and have an adequate range of options to choose from. Raz offers the following examples[8] to illustrate these positive requirements:

> The Man in the Pit: A person falls down a pit and remains there the rest of his life, unable to climb out or to summon help. There is just enough ready food to keep him alive without (after he gets used to it) any suffering. He can do nothing much, not even move much. His choices are confined to whether to eat now or a little later, whether to sleep now or a little later, whether to scratch his left ear or not.

> The Hounded Woman: A person finds herself on a small desert island. She shares the island with a fierce carnivorous animal which perpetually hunts for her. Her mental stamina, her intellectual ingenuity, her will power and her physical resources are taxed to their limits by her struggle to remain alive. She never has a chance to do or even think of anything other than how to escape from the beast.

In the above examples, the absence of positive factors (such as an adequate range of options to choose from) seem to undermine the agent's ability to determine for herself what action to engage in. While in both examples the agent enjoys negative liberty, it seems inappropriate to describe each agent's action in terms of self-determination. Autonomy requires something more than mere negative liberty. In fact, the stability and ensuing predictability provided by authority as discussed by Dorsey and Hayek seem to be such positive characteristics needed for self-determination. When Hayek states that the law allows a person to act effectively on her own knowledge, he does not mean that the law removes obstacles to my acting on my knowledge (although in many cases the law does protect this "negative liberty"). Hayek refers to the positive resource of stability which enables the agent to effectively predict the results of his action and base his determination of action upon this knowledge.

Berlin characterizes such conceptions in terms of positive liberty, which he says "derives from the wish on the part of the individual to be his own master,"[9] and not simply react to external forces:

> I wish to be a subject, not an object; to be moved by reasons, by conscious purposes, which are my own, not by causes which affect me, as it were, from outside.[10]

Thus, the effect external influences have on autonomy is central to its practical function. A practical conception of autonomy needs to show how an agent is able to be influenced by external factors and retain a sense of positively determining her own behavior.

I shall argue that there are two fundamentally different approaches to the notion of autonomy and the metaphysical grounds upon which the concept is developed. I shall call these approaches the notion of 'autonomy as autarkeia' and the notion of 'autonomy as self-rule' respectively. These two opposing conceptions of autonomy take different positions on the effect of external influences upon the autonomy of an agent. Wherein the notion of 'autonomy as autarkeia' views "external" factors as incompatible with autonomy, the concept of 'autonomy as self-rule' allows external factors to influence the determination of action without eliminating the autonomy of the agent.

I will argue that the conception of 'autonomy as autarkeia' is too rigorous, and that our understanding of autonomy should be conceptualized in terms of 'autonomy as self-rule'. This approach to autonomy can serve a much more practical function than the notion of autarkeia which autonomy is usually associated with, for several reasons. One, it allows a fuller range of actions to be considered autonomous. As we shall see, action stemming from love or altruism would likely fail the requirement of self-sufficiency required by the notion of 'autonomy as autarkeia'. The conception of 'autonomy as self-rule' may allow a person to act for such "external" purposes without sacrificing her autonomy.

Secondly, the conception of 'autonomy as self-rule' allows for appeals to authority in areas of life in which we lack competence. We, as the "helmsmen" of our own lives, steer toward various forms of authority in certain facets of life, and away from authority in others. We are not self-sufficient, but this does not mean that we do not "rule" our own lives. In this way, the notion of autonomy can be developed as a practical notion for individuals living within the structure of a political and social system.

I. AUTONOMY AS AUTARKEIA

Autarkeia in Aristotle

Let us first examine the grounding of the view of "autonomy as self sufficiency", so that we may better understand the contrast of this view with the concept of autonomy we shall develop. For Aristotle self-sufficiency, or "autarkeia", is the primary good and chief aim of a city-state:

> Again, the object for which a thing exists, its end, is its chief good; and self sufficiency is an end, and a chief good. (Pol.1253a1-2).

While Aristotle recognizes the role played by both the individual's need for social cooperation in order to survive, as well as the desire to interact socially as important reasons for the formation of political society (EE 1242a7-9)[11], he concludes that the final cause and end of political society is not mere companionship (Pol. 1281a5)[12], but rather is to achieve self-sufficiency (Pol. 1252b30-1253a). This self-sufficiency consists in being independent from outside powers, in that the city-state provides all that is necessary to flourish:

> the self-sufficient we now define as that which when isolated makes life desirable and lacking in nothing. (EN 1097b15).

The concept of autarkeia is developed in several works by Aristotle. While most widely recognized and clearly developed in relation to the city-state, E.B. Cole finds there are at least two other contexts in which the idea of self-sufficiency is developed.[13] These are in relation to friendship, and in relation to the "great-souled man". There seem to be common elements in each development of the concept of self-sufficiency, and these common elements are what I shall take as the essence of "autarkeia".

In the context of friendship, Cole finds self-sufficient friendship to be contrasted with friendship which is based upon some service or favor which the friendship can provide, and with friendship which is based upon one's need for "amusement and society".[14] Through this contrast, Cole concludes that autarkeia in friendship denotes a degree of independence in which the friendship is not entered into in order to fill some perceived lacking, "For it does not belong to the self-sufficing man to need either useful friends or friends to amuse him and society, for he is sufficient society for himself." (EE 1244b6ff.). A self-sufficient person does not look beyond himself to fill a perceived lacking.

The concern in regard to external influences over one's ability to flourish is also apparent in Aristotle's concept of the "great-souled man". For this type of man, self-sufficiency consists in choosing what one will pursue without the pressure of need or utility being a relevant determinant of choice. Cole finds Aristotle to hold the position that the pursuit of the beautiful and profitless, rather than the profitable and useful, is more proper to a character that is self-sufficient.[15] Again, to choose on the basis of usefulness is to choose in order to fulfil an external purpose. A self-sufficient man does not look beyond himself for this purpose.

The common features of self-sufficiency seem to be that the self-sufficient is one who pursues ends not determined by some external purpose or perceived lacking in what is needed to flourish. Autarkeia, then, is independence from external influences (such as need or utility).

Autarkeia in Kant

The influence of the concept of autarkeia can be seen in modern conceptions of autonomy. While Immanuel Kant does not focus on the idea of political society in his discussion of autonomy,[16] the underlying emphasis on self-sufficiency, and independence from external influences over human flourishing, is clearly the central concern for Kant as well. More recently, conceptions of autonomy presented by Joel Feinberg,[17] John Rawls[18] and Robert Paul Wolff[19] (as well as others) all center around the idea that external influences pose a threat in some form to human autonomy.

Kant discussed autonomy in terms of man's moral character, and so was concerned with man's control over the moral value of his actions. Thus, his discussion of autonomy does not center upon the practical determination of action, but upon the formal determination of the moral value of action. Kant's conception of autonomy, however, has influenced modern accounts of the autonomous determination of practical action, which have taken the Kantian idea of moral autonomy and developed notions of autonomous practical reasoning in Kantian terms. Thus it will pay to examine Kant's conception of autonomy in detail, so that we can understand its inadequacy as a conception of autonomous practical determinations of action.

Kant begins the Grounding by asserting the nature of the good to be identified with the "good will". He explains that other "goods", such as intelligence, strength, etc. are not "good in themselves", but rather depend for their goodness upon their use by a good will.[20] Intelligence, for example, is only good if it is not employed by an evil will to accomplish rather dastardly deeds. In this way the moral value of such things as intelligence are dependent upon contingent "external" considerations, particularly the presence of a good will.

The presence of the good will, however, is not dependent upon external considerations for its moral value. The good will is good "in itself". In order to maintain this moral value, the will should not subjugate itself to contingent, external factors. Moral value should be tied to the will alone. Thus, the will should not be influenced by external factors in determining duty:

> Autonomy of the will is the property the will has of being a law to itself (independently of any property of the objects of volition).[21]

If external considerations are allowed to effect moral value, the determination of duty becomes a contingent matter, subject to the contingencies of external circumstance, etc. (much as the value of things such as 'intelligence' was dependent upon its use by a good will in Kant's earlier examples). For example, if my principle of action[22] only has moral value when certain circumstances are present, my principle of action depends for its moral value upon the presence of these circumstances, just as intelligence depends for its "goodness" upon its use by a good will. In eliminating these considerations from the determination of moral value, the agent regains control over the moral value of his actions. Thus, moral value should be determined a priori:

> It is clear from the foregoing that all moral concepts have their seat and origin completely a priori in reason, and indeed in the most ordinary human reason just as much as in the most highly speculative. They cannot be ab-

stracted from any empirical, and hence merely contingent, cognition. In this purity of their origin lies their very worthiness to serve us as supreme practical principles; and to the extent that something empirical is added to them, just so much is taken away from their genuine influence and from the absolute worth of the corresponding actions.[23]

Moral value is tied to pure (a priori) reason in order to eliminate the contingencies of circumstance, etc. (Kant calls these considerations "alien causes"). In this, the moral value of an action is not determined by reference to the particular circumstance in which it is performed, or by reference to some result which is to be achieved. The moral value of the action is contained in the principle of action itself (for Kant, the "maxim of choice"). Moral value is *self sufficient*, independent of considerations such as usefulness, desire, etc. (the very considerations which Aristotle conceives of autarkeia as ignoring).

To achieve this a priori purity, Kant offers the following "principle of autonomy":

> The principle of autonomy is this: Always choose in such a way that in the same volition the maxims of choice are at the same time present as universal law.[24]

Kant's doctrine of universalizability is a test of self-sufficiency; a test to determine if the moral value of a potential duty is dependent upon "external" factors. If a maxim (or principle of action; again, I use these interchangeably) can be universalized, it is independent of reference to specific empirical contingencies, and thus is self-sufficient. However, if the maxim cannot be universalized, it is dependent for its moral value on the contingent presence of the circumstances and conditions within which it would apply.

The principle of autonomy (which is based upon the doctrine of universalizability) is a strategy for making moral determinations, which is designed to make the moral determination self-sufficient. By making the determination solely on the basis of universal laws, one does not (morally) act to achieve some purpose in a particular circumstance, but rather acts because one's moral duty is valuable in and of itself; it does not depend for its moral value upon the contingent presence of anything "external".

In this way, moral value is contained in the *formulation* of the moral determination, rather than its content. The specific content of the duty in particular circumstances might make reference to empirical contingencies (and not be self-sufficient), but the formulation of moral duty makes no such empirical references. For example, take a potential duty to develop one's talents. I may need to take into account the fact that I have athletic talents but not musical talents in order to know what this duty would require in action (the actual content of the duty for me). The actual *content* of my duty (if in fact it is a duty) is **not** a self-sufficient determination, free of reference to empirical contingencies (such as the empirical fact that I have athletic talents). But the determination that developing talents is a moral duty rests upon the test of self-sufficiency. If the maxim "develop one's talents" is formulated independently of empirical contingencies (it is morally valuable in and of itself), it qualifies as self-sufficient (and thus qualifies to be a moral duty).

In the above, we can see that moral autonomy is achieved through the self-sufficient *formulation* of one's principles of action, rather than the self-sufficient determination of the content of one's action. Lewis White Beck describes Kant's project in this way:

> What he is establishing, as we have said, is a principle of categorical imperatives, a formula, a second-order principle, and not an imperative for specific action.[25]

As we shall see in a few pages, this formal notion of autonomy simply seems too rigorous to serve as a conception we can use to describe the autonomous determination of an agent's action. A notion of autonomy rooted in such a conception of self-sufficiency is threatened by authority, or any form of "external" consideration. On this view, autonomy requires the will determine duty in a self-sufficient manner.

This Kantian view of moral autonomy as autarkeia has been very influential in the many modern discussions of autonomy. The Kantian conception of moral autonomy has been applied to practical and other uses of the term. This influence is apparent in the following discussion of the term's modern uses, taken from Joel Feinberg's <u>Harm to Self</u>:

> When applied to individuals the word "autonomy" has four closely related meanings. It can refer either to the <u>capacity</u> to govern oneself, which of course is a matter of degree; or to the <u>actual condition</u> of self-government and its associated virtues; or to an <u>ideal of character</u> derived from that conception; or (on the analogy of the political state) to the <u>sovereign authority</u> to govern oneself, which is absolute within one's own moral boundaries (one's "territory", "realm", "sphere", or "domain"). Note that corresponding to these senses of "autonomous" there are parallel senses of the term "independent": The <u>capacity</u> to support oneself, direct ones own life, and be finally responsible for one's own decisions; the <u>de facto condition</u> of self-sufficiency, which consists in the exercise of the appropriate capacities when the circumstances permit; the ideal of self-sufficiency; and the sense, applied mainly to political states, of <u>de jure sovereignty</u> and the right of self-determination.[26]

Although Feinberg claims that there are four (closely related) meanings to the term "autonomy", there is nothing in his claim to reject the idea that there is a core concept which lies at the heart of the notion of autonomy.[27] It is apparent from his assertion that there are four corresponding notions of "independent" (which he seems to take as a form of self-sufficiency) that such a concept could qualify as a "core concept".

That the idea of self-sufficiency could be seen as a core concept is particularly plausible when one considers that the emphasis on self-sufficiency is especially stressed in Feinberg's discussion of autonomy as an "actual condition" and as an "ideal of character". This is important, since it seems that it is the actual condition of autonomy which the other uses of autonomy revolve around. For example, a capacity for autonomy is a capacity to realize the actual condition of autonomy; The sovereign authority, or right to autonomy is a right to the actual condition of self-government; and the ideal of character is described by Feinberg as derived from the actual condition of autonomy. Thus, the "actual condition" of autonomy seems to play a central role in all four concepts, and thus the emphasis on self-sufficiency here should carry over to the other concepts as well (Hence, Feinberg's recognition that a notion of "independent" corresponds to each use of autonomy).

The fact that current uses of the term "autonomy" reflect the ideal of `autonomy as autarkeia' should come as no surprise, as the most influential writings on the concept in recent years reflect this outlook. The most influential of modern writers on this subject have probably been John Rawls[28] and Robert Paul Wolff[29]. The works of these writers have had a tremendous effect upon the discussion of autonomy and its proper applications.

Rawls in particular shares the Kantian view of inclinations, inhibitions, circumstances and the like as foreign to the "self", as evidenced by the following passage:

> Imagine then that someone experiences the promptings of his moral sense as inexplicable inhibitions which for the moment he is unable to justify. Why should he not regard them as simply neurotic compulsions? If it should turn out that these scruples are indeed largely shaped and accounted for by the contingencies of early childhood, perhaps by the course of family history and class situation...then there is surely no reason why they should govern our lives.[30]

Rawls believes that one's life should be governed by considered judgments which are "independent of natural contingencies and accidental circumstances"[31], and maintains that autonomous individuals should thus govern their lives according to justice, which requires that people test their action against principles adopted behind the "veil of ignorance",[32] which is defined as follows:

> Among the essential features of this situation is that no one knows his place in society, his class position or social status, nor does any one know his fortune in the distribution of natural assets and abilities, his intelligence, strength and the like. I shall even assume that the parties do not know their conceptions of the good or their special psychological propensities. The principles of justice are chosen behind a veil of ignorance.[33]

By not allowing agents to have knowledge of their personal endowments, desires, projects and inclinations, the veil of ignorance keeps people from governing their lives according to principles which contain these contingent, "external" considerations.

Robert Paul Wolff, in his book <u>In Defense of Anarchism</u>,[34] draws out the political implications for the Kantian notion of autonomy. Wolff does not offer a metaphysical theory of the "self"; instead, he concentrates on the use of "autonomy" in terms of what Feinberg refers to as "sovereign authority", and thus describes autonomy in its political form. Autonomy is freedom from the control of another's will, and this freedom, along with the obligation to acknowledge this freedom in taking responsibility for one's action, leads Wolff to conclude that autonomy is simply incompatible with binding commands from an authority. <u>Autonomous</u> action must be determined by the agent alone.[35] When, for example, we place ourselves in the hands of a physician, we give up our autonomy (albeit justifiably).[36] States Wolff:

> The autonomous man, insofar as he is autonomous, is not subject to the will of another. He may do what another tells him, but not <u>because</u> he has been told to do it.[37]

As we shall see in chapter six, to recognize authority is to comply with the directives of authority <u>because</u> the authority directed it. Thus, autonomy and authority are, by Wolff's model, simply incompatible.

The Inadequacy of Autarkeia for Practical Autonomy

The problem with the view of autonomy as self-sufficiency is that it is too rigorous for practical application. While self-sufficiency in determining moral value may seem enticing, it is all but impossible at the level of practical determinations of action. Even Wolff recognizes this:

> There are great, perhaps insurmountable, obstacles to the achievement of a complete and rational autonomy in the modern world.[38]

To act in a self-sufficient manner seems a rather austere existence, lacking many of the things we think to be a part of a full, rich and robust life. To act for such contingent, external purposes as fulfilling the wishes of a child, spouse or parent <u>because</u> it is what the loved-one wishes would not meet the requirement of self-sufficiency, for the determination of action would then be contingent upon the content of the loved-one's wishes (and thus not self sufficient). Yet such actions are often what we consider the very embodiment of a rich life.[39]

In addition, there appears to be a fundamental incompatibility between self-sufficiency and any appeal to authority. If the determination of one's action depends upon the content of the decree of an authority, the determination of action is not self-sufficient. However, appeals to various forms of authority are an everyday part of life. For example, we appeal to the authority of the physician in medicine, to the scientist in physics, and to the traffic laws when driving. Far from being a threat to autonomy, these appeals to authority seem to broaden our autonomy. We could scarcely get from one place to another if there were not a general conformity to the traffic laws, for example. And appeals to authority in areas such as medicine allow us to be free from learning basic skills in this area if we so wish, and to decide to spend this time developing competencies in other areas.

The rigor of the notion of 'autonomy as autarkeia' simply seems too great. To be a practical notion, autonomy must allow that a person be able to incorporate external influences into his determination of action, rather than requiring complete detachment from them. It is just this which is achieved by a notion of autonomy as 'self-rule'.

II. AUTONOMY AS SELF-RULE

Thus far, I have examined how the modern concept of autonomy has developed along the lines of autarkeia, or self-sufficiency. However, John Macken[40] shows that the term 'autonomy' was first employed by the Greeks to denote certain rights of a city-state (to manage its own affairs) even when dependent on a mother-city or outside power. Macken traces the idea of autonomy through the Enlightenment, when 'autonomy' was used to refer to the rights of individuals to manage their own affairs within the limits of a larger framework set by law. Such a use of 'autonomy' seems at odds with the concept of self-sufficiency or <u>autarkeia</u> as developed since Kant, and raises questions about the proper notions which underlie the concept of autonomy.

'Autonomy' is derived from the Greek words <u>autos</u> and <u>nomos</u> meaning, literally, "self-rule". To gain a better understanding of the proper roots of this term, we must delve into an understanding of "rulers" in Greek philosophy. Aristotle analyzed the ruler in terms of the Greek city-state. In the <u>Politics</u>, Aristotle compares citizens to sailors on a ship:

> Like the sailor, the citizen is a member of a community.
> Now, sailors have different functions, for one of them is
> a rower, another a pilot, and third a look-out man, a fourth
> is described by some similar term... (Pol.1276b20-25)

The ruler is as the pilot, or helmsman of the ship (Pol.1279a1-5). Within the context of the city-state, the ruler alone possesses the characteristic of practical wisdom, and it is this which distinguishes him from the ordinary citizen (Pol.1277b25-30). In possessing practical wisdom, the ruler determines what should be done.

It is no coincidence that Aristotle uses the analogy of a helmsman, for the helmsman of a ship steers the ship within the context of "external" considerations (such as whether it is empirically possible to turn a certain direction, what the weather and currents are like, etc.). To understand practical wisdom in Aristotle is to understand determination of virtuous action as involving a guide to action in relation to the "external" considerations of one's own capabilities and characteristics, as well as the situation at hand. Practical wisdom determines virtuous action, but does so in the context of the circumstances of the individual. This has become known as the "mean".[41]

The feature which stands out most in the context of our examination of autonomy thus far is how Aristotle views the role of practical reason and the "law of reason" in the determination of moral value, and how this differs from Kant's view. Kant held that moral value should be pure, uninfluenced by external considerations. For this reason, "alien causes" are eliminated from effecting the moral value of action; thus the moral value of a particular action becomes as consistent of a determination as a mathematical deduction (it does not depend on circumstances, the individual person, etc.).

Aristotle, on the other hand, recognized that the determination of virtuous action is practical; such determinations are not of the precise nature of theoretical reasoning (EN1104a5-10). The moral value of particular actions vary from situation to situation, and from person to person. Thus, Aristotle views the law of practical reason in relation to moral duty to be embodied in the mean, which incorporates external considerations into the very core of the determination of moral duty:

> But this must be agreed upon before hand, that the whole account of matters of conduct must be given in outline and not precisely, as we said at the very beginning that the accounts we demand must be in accordance with the subject-matter; matters concerned with conduct and questions of what is good for us have no fixity, any more than matters of health. The general account being of this nature, the account of particular cases is yet more lacking

in exactness; for they do not fall under any art or precept but the agents themselves must in each case consider what is appropriate to the occasion, as happens also in the art of medicine or <u>of navigation</u> (EN 1104a1-10 Emphasis added).

In this Aristotelian sense, external influences are not viewed as a threat to one's ability to rule, so long as one acts according to practical wisdom rather than some other determinant of behavior (such as allowing desires to steer one to indulge in every pleasure). A ruler is as a helmsman of a ship, and steers according to practical wisdom (in the form of the mean). Should external influences become the determinant of behavior, those external influences act as helmsman, and as ruler.

External influences must not <u>determine</u> behavior; so long as they do not rule, but merely affect how one rules (by affecting the "mean" as currents or weather would affect a ship's helmsman), they pose no threat to one's ability to <u>rule</u> one's own life. The issue is one of who is helmsman; the agent, or the "external factors"?

But it is precisely here that Kant rejects this notion of autonomy as "helmsmanship". Kant feared that in allowing external considerations to influence the determination of moral worth, man became subject to the external forces which dictated various consequences; he feared that since external considerations dictated action, they acted as "helmsman". Thus, Kant developed a concept of "autonomy as autarkeia" which extinguished the control of external influences over the determination of moral worth.

I believe that Kant's fears in this regard can be traced to a specific conception of external influences, in which the various considerations which enter into an agent's determinations act as "causes". When external factors (for Kant, "alien causes") are allowed to effect the moral value of action, the agent's own cognitive judgments are relegated to determining the most virtuous contingencies established by the external factors, and thus the determination of moral value reflects more the external factors than the agent's own assessments.

Likewise, the application of the Kantian conception of moral autonomy to practical realms shares this view of external influences. Social pressure, authority etc. are viewed as *causes* of behavior, and when they are allowed to enter the determination of action the agent is relegated to a subservient, passive role of reacting to these influences.

In the following chapters, I shall examine in much greater depth the conception of autonomy based upon the metaphor of the helmsman. This model of autonomy can provide a practical standard of autonomous action. We may allow, for example, that an agent is subject to the influence of advertising, argument, or hierarchy without necessarily sacrificing his autonomy. We may allow a sick person to appeal to a physician and retain his autonomy. Indeed, the steering toward authority in the area of medical care and away in some other area is the very embodiment of autonomy. It is this notion of autonomy as self-rule which must be recognized if we are to use the concept in a viable way for practical purposes.

I shall also examine Kant's fears concerning external influences, and show that these fears can be overcome with a proper understanding of human motivation. Desires and other external influences do not cause behavior in the manner Kant posited. An adequate model of human motivation must posit an active role for the agent.

[1] See Feinberg, Joel Harm to Self (New York: Oxford University Press, 1986).
[2] Dworkin, Gerald The Theory and Practice of Autonomy (New York: Cambridge University Press, 1988), p.6.
[3] See Dorsey, Gray Lankford "The Necessity of Authority to Freedom"; Hendel, Charles W. "Freedom and Authority as Functions of Civilization"; and Bokser, Ben Zion "Freedom and Authority"; all in Freedom and Authority in Our Time: Twelfth Symposium on Science, Philosophy and Religion (New York, Harper and Brothers, 1953).
[4] Dorsey, Gray Lankford "The Necessity of Authority to Freedom".
[5] Hayek, F.A. The Constitution of Liberty, (University of Chicago Press, 1960), pp.156-157.
[6] Berlin, Four Essays on Liberty, p.122.
[7] Raz, Joseph The Morality of Freedom, (New York: Oxford University Press, 1986), p.372.
[8] Raz, The Morality of Freedom, pp.373-374.
[9] Berlin, Four Essays on Liberty, p.131.
[10] Berlin, Four Essays on Liberty, p.131.

[11] For References to the EE, I use The Complete Works of Aristotle, ed. by Jonathan Barnes, (Princeton: Bollingen, 1984).

[12] For References to the EN and Pol., I use The Basic Works of Aristotle, ed. by Richard McKeon (NY: Random House, 1941).

[13] Cole, E.B., "'Autarkeia' in Aristotle", University of Dayton Review, Vol.19, No.3 (Winter 1988-89), pp.35-42.

[14] Cole, "'Autarkeia' in Aristotle", p.36.

[15] Cole, "'Autarkeia' in Aristotle", p.38.

[16] Kant, Immanuel Grounding for the Metaphysics of Morals, trans. by James W. Ellington, Hackett Publishing Co., 1981).

[17] Feinberg, Joel, Harm to Self (New York: Oxford University Press, 1986).

[18] Rawls, John A Theory of Justice (Cambridge: Harvard University Press, 1971).

[19] Wolff, Robert Paul, In Defense of Anarchism (New York: Harper and Row, 1970).

[20] Kant, Grounding for the Metaphysics of Morals, p.7.

[21] Kant, Grounding for the Metaphysics of Morals, p.44.

[22] I shall use "principle of action" in a way which for our purposes is identical to Kant's "maxim of choice".

[23] Kant, Grounding for the Metaphysics of Morals, pp.22-23.

[24] Kant, Grounding for the Metaphysics of Morals, p.44.

[25] Beck, Lewis White, "Apodictic Imperatives" in Wolff, Robert Paul (ed.), Kant: Foundations of the Metaphysics of Morals (Text and Critical Essays) (Bobbs-Merrill Company, Inc., 1969), p.147.

[26] Feinberg, Joel Harm to Self (New York: Oxford University Press, 1986), p.28.

[27] See Christman, John The Inner Citadel (New York: Oxford University Press, 1989), pp.5-6. Although I differ with Christman concerning what this core concept is, I owe to him the recognition that a core concept is a possibility in Feinberg's account.

[28] Rawls, John A Theory of Justice (Cambridge: Harvard University Press, 1971).

[29] Wolff, Robert Paul In Defense of Anarchism

[30] Rawls, A Theory of Justice, p.514.

[31] Rawls, A Theory of Justice, p.515.

[32] While Rawls has, since writing A Theory of Justice, retreated from metaphysical conclusions (see, for example, "Justice as Fairness: Political Not Metaphysical", Philosophy and Public Affairs, vol.14 (1985), pp.223-251), there remains a question concerning whether such a retreat is possible given his desert-based argument that the natural lottery undermines a view that justice can be based upon those characteristics which are acquired by "luck". Regardless of whether or not Rawls' retreat is valid, the discussion of autonomy (pp.510-515) seems incontestably tied to metaphysical conceptions of self, and at least has been taken as such in recent discussions on moral luck and moral responsibility. I therefore examine Rawls' views in the context of their impact upon metaphysical discussions of the self and moral responsi-

bility, ignoring Rawls' retreat from metaphysical conclusions.

[33] Rawls, A Theory of Justice, p.12.

[34] Wolff, Robert Paul In Defense of Anarchism (New York: Harper and Row, 1970).

[35] Wolff, In Defense of Anarchism, p.13.

[36] Wolff, In Defense of Anarchism, p.15.

[37] Wolff, In Defense of Anarchism, p.14.

[38] Wolff, In Defense of Anarchism, p.17.

[39] For a good discussion of how many modern notions of practical autonomy are at odds with such behavior, see Dworkin, Gerald The Theory and Practice of Autonomy (New York: Cambridge University Press, 1988), pp.23-25.

[40] See John Macken, S.J., The Autonomy Theme in the Church Dogmatics (New York: Cambridge University Press, 1990).

[41] Aristotle's mean is a theory of practical wisdom which guides us to act in given circumstances according to virtue. This involves acting without excess or deficiency in regard to the situation at hand. For example, in a battlefield situation, I should not act in cowardice, but neither should I act in a foolhardy manner. I should assess the situation, identify what is cowardly, what is foolhardy, and act somewhere in between.

Of course, exactly what is foolhardy and what is cowardly will differ from situation to situation, and from person to person. It may be quite reasonable for a trained Navy Seal, for example, to attempt to infiltrate enemy lines. However, a novice at wartime experience would be foolhardy to attempt such a thing. On the other hand, it might be considered cowardly for a strapping young man to stand idly by as a woman is beaten in front of him, while it would be perfectly reasonable for a little old lady to avoid becoming involved in the altercation.

CHAPTER THREE:
Developing the Helmsman Metaphor

The concept of "autonomy as self-rule" that I argued for in the preceding chapter is a concept of autonomy grounded in an understanding of the determination of action along the lines of the "helmsman" metaphor. In making the shift from formal concerns to substantive, the view of autonomy under the metaphor of the helmsman shifts the focus of the concept from "independence" or "self-sufficiency" to that of active evaluative assessment. Autonomy does not require detachment from external influences. Rather, it requires that the agent actively assess these influences rather than simply react to them. External influences do not *cause* action, but rather provide information (facts) which the agent, as "helmsman", then steers according to. This understanding of autonomy in terms of acting as helmsman of one's own behavior requires more specific development. How can we distinguish when a person does and does not act as "helmsman"?

The answer to the above question cannot be given in terms of an analytical distinction involving criteria which must be met for "autonomy" to apply. Rather, we must examine the behavior in question and ask who, or what, seems to have acted as "helmsman". This standard of autonomy is admittedly sometimes fuzzy. There will no doubt exist controversy about whether the action in question reflects the agent's active assessment, or the various influences at hand. This fuzziness, however, occurs in terms which are clearly identifiable (namely, whether the agent acted as helmsman), and thus debate can take place along identifiable lines. That is, the "fuzziness" in question does not concern what the concept itself consists of, but rather concerns epistemic problems raised in the application of the concept to actual behavior.

In this, the fuzziness of the concept does not present the problems I identified with the concept of autonomy in the first chapter: it is able to serve a viable role in applied ethics. This is so because the controversies surrounding the concept are not controversies about how the concept itself is used (as Feinberg describes the concept's problems for applied purposes), or controversies surrounding a vague "term of art" (as Dworkin proposed). Rather, the controversies concern epistemic difficulties which, as we shall see below, can be addressed for practical purposes. Thus, the fuzziness in question does not threaten our ability to understand, in the abstract, what we are debating. We are debating the application of a consistent conceptual apparatus: we are debating whether the agent should be considered the "helmsman" of her behavior.

The application of the concept of autonomy is often fuzzy because epistemically, identifying who (or what) steers the determination of behavior itself is often fuzzy. Different influences affect different agents to different degrees. Many agents seem to be *in part* compelled, and *in part* helmsman of their behavior. But these "fuzzy" situations pose no threat to autonomy understood in terms of the helmsman metaphor. Autonomy is a concept which admits of degrees. Some influences steer certain aspects of an agent's behavior, while she remains helmsman in regard to the majority of the aspects of her behavior (we will look at examples of this as the chapter progresses). When this happens, the agent is *less autonomous* than an agent who steers every aspect of her behavior. Any concept which admits of degree in this way is subject to fuzziness in application to the world.

Even though the application of the concept of autonomy to the actual world is sometimes fuzzy, we **do** make determinations of when autonomy applies, and we **do** ascribe moral responsibility on this basis (as well as diminish moral responsibility to the degree that autonomy does not apply). How we do this is by no means perfect, but it is remarkably effective in practice. The imperfections of the practice are imperfections which face *any* third-person evaluation of an agent's first-person assessments or intentions.

The problems arise when we ask from what perspective autonomy should be understood. If it is a third-person perspective, autonomy seems too "objective" in that it does not seem to center around the particular agent in question. But if it is purely a first-person perspective, then *any* action which results from an agent's assessment seems autonomous. If the helmsman metaphor is to be taken seriously, there might be times when action results from an agent's assessment, but the agent does not "steer" this assessment. Coerced behavior, for example, results from an assessment of the agent who is coerced, yet is a paradigm instance of non-autonomous behavior. A *purely* first-person perspective will have trouble accounting for this.

Autonomy must center around the particular agent in question. But determining who steers behavior must also involve some reference to more objective standards. If an agent acts to cause great damage under threat of a disapproving look, we consider them autonomous even though they might claim they were coerced. Conversely, when a paranoid schizophrenic acts on the basis of paranoid delusions, we do not recognize autonomy though she might claim it. Autonomous agents act for reasons which result from *their* assessment of various considerations and influences. But a more objective perspective must place **boundaries** on the first-person assessments which are said to reflect autonomy. How these boundaries are established shall be the focus of this chapter.

Writers such as Alan Gibbard have attempted to address this problem by drawing a distinction between "rationality" and "advisability". According to Gibbard, "Acting in full awareness of the facts suggests not rationality, but something more like 'advisability'"[1]. Gibbard's distinction seems to draw upon the relevant facts which the agent is aware of, making "rationality" apply to the facts which the agent is *in fact* aware of, and "advisability" apply to all the facts which the agent *might have been* aware of. Gibbard states that "Whereas rationality is a matter of making use of the information one has, advice can draw on information one lacks".[2] The relationship between these suggests that it is improper to use a third-person standard to assess the rationality of first-person agency. This is because the third-person perspective is simply not applicable to the actual first-person situation of the agent in question. Rather, the relationship between them seems one of priority, the "rational" agent attempting to approximate, as best she can given her local (imperfect) knowledge, what would be rational from a third-person perspective. But assessing the rationality of action on the basis of reasons which the agent does not *in fact* take herself to have (perhaps because she is unaware of them) is inappropriate. States Gibbard:

> Of course, once I have his advice, it then becomes rational for me to do what he says - but only then. Rationality, we may conclude, is related to advisability, but the connection is this: in the special case in which I know all

that bears on my choice, what it is rational for me to do is what it is advisable for me to do."[3]

This understanding of the relationship between rationality from the first- and third-person perspectives seems popular.[4] However, it seems to miss the way we actually relate rationality from the two perspectives. Take a paranoid schizophrenic. We do not simply look at his action and its relationship to the reasons *he took himself to have* to assess his action's rationality. To use Gibbard's terminology (though not his view of this relationship), we do not say that his action was "rational", but not "advisable". rather, we deem his action *irrational*, and the irrationality of his action is assessed in part through its consistency with boundaries established by the third-person perspective. Was it sane? Are his reasons for action of the type which we understand people as able to take? We shall take up both of these questions in detail in a few pages. For now, though, the important point is that the third-person perspective is used to assess in part the first-person rationality of action.

The use of third-person evaluations to assess the first-person rationality of action raises many practical difficulties. A person's exclusive access to her "reasons for action" poses epistemic problems. How can we assess the rationality of an agent's reasons for action if we cannot know what her reasons for action were? As we shall see, this epistemic problem requires the practical use of certain devices for understanding what reasons an agent likely has acted for. While these devices are not perfect, pragmatically they serve to address this *practical* problem. That we make third-person evaluations of an agent's first-person assessments can be seen clearly in the example of criminal trials. Here, a jury considers various descriptions of an agent's first-person intentions, assessments and motives, and decides which seems to best fit the case in question. In making these evaluations, there is often disagreement within the jury. In fact, there are sometimes cases when a "hung jury" is unable to decide. But in the vast majority of cases, a determination **is** made.

Many of the standards used by juries to make these third-person evaluations of an agent's first-person assessments are very similar to the standards we shall discuss for making third-person evaluations of first-person autonomy in this chapter. Previous patterns of assessment, the viability of options, and the reasonableness of acting otherwise (in the form of a "sensible man" standard, which we shall take up below) are important components both in determining the agent's assessments, and whether the behavior in question reflects an autonomous assessment at all.

The problems, however, do not stop here. Once an agent's reasons for action are identified, how do we assess the "sanity" of them? As we shall see below, this requires an understanding of the types of creatures which human beings are, and the array of reasons which a "reasonable person" might act for. Just as the helmsman steers according to practical wisdom in Aristotle, the autonomous agent must possess the capacity to make reasonable assessments in order to steer behavior. "Correct" reasoning here does not indicate *a particular* correct determination of action, but does specify a boundary within which autonomous action must fall.

Just as practical wisdom in Aristotle's work is relative to the particular agent, our conception of "reasonable" behavior does not point to a uniquely "rational" decision. It is simply wrong to assume that, given a particular circumstance, *any* agent would reach a particular decision if she were "reasonable". What is reasonable in any situation depends upon the unique goals, aspirations, prior experiences, and particular limitations (epistemic, mental, and physical) of the agent in question, as well as her tendencies to assess certain things as more important than others. But the "reasonable person" standard does set boundaries on the types of decisions which might be understood as "reasonable". Autonomous action is bounded by a conception of competence which allows the agent to actually steer behavior according to the influences and circumstances present. Psychological incompetence ("insanity"), for example, may threaten this capacity to steer, and thus threaten the application of autonomy. Additionally, human nature itself places boundaries upon the types of assessments which "reasonable" human beings might make. We shall take this up in detail under our discussion of the justification of a "sensible man" standard, and our discussion of the conditions of autonomy, below.

In this chapter, I will develop the metaphor of the helmsman as a basis for understanding autonomy. I will offer a number of guides to identify when an agent acts as helmsman and when she does not. These guides identify autonomy through the agent's contribution to the determination of action, and our ascription to the agent's judgement of the explanation as to why a particular action occurred. These ways to identify autonomous action should not be taken as exhaustive, however; nor should they be taken as a specification of the criteria for autonomous action. As I stated at the beginning of this chapter, the concept of autonomy understood in terms of the helmsman metaphor cannot be developed under a set of "criteria". The discussion of autonomy contained in this chapter should be taken as a "guide" for identifying when an agent acts as helmsman, and not as criteria.

Identifying Helmsmanship

The first point which demands attention in developing the helmsman metaphor concerns the level at which we should understand both autonomy and responsibility for the purposes of applied ethics and the organization of society. The concept of autonomy should be understood at the level of **action**, and not in terms of the will. In this, it differs from the understanding of autonomy as offered in models by theorists like Gerald Dworkin.[5]

The view of autonomy as self-rule is a substantive notion of autonomy. Autonomy requires that the agent play an active role in formulating the *content* of her behavior. Thus, it is concerned with *the determination of action by the agent*, and not with formal questions about *how the agent herself is determined*. We shall take this up in much greater detail in chapter four, when we discuss a key distinction between freedom of action and freedom of will.

Recall our discussion of autonomy and personal identity in chapter one. There, I argued that our identity is tied to autonomous actions, providing examples of how a lack of autonomy leads to a lack of identification with behavior (such as in cases of coercion). The identifying characteristic of autonomy is the agent's active assessment. What we mean when we say that a person has autonomy is that she does not simply react to her environment and other influences, but actively shapes her behavior in the context of them. It is this active assessment which lends identity to the behavior as a particular agent's action, ascribable to her active assessment of present influences in a way that a passive reaction is not.

This is why certain patterns of behavior and tendencies to evaluate circumstances in a particular way, are indicative that a particular behavior is Joan's. It is when a particular behavior does not fall into a pattern which we recognize as reflecting the assessments of various facts which Joan usually makes, that we begin to worry that the behavior does not reflect Joan's autonomous determination of action. This is because it is behavior which reflects the active assessment which Joan makes of various influences that we ascribe to Joan, because it is her active assessment which accounts for why she behaved in the way she did.

Furthermore, it is when behavior is reflective of a particular assessment which is *unique* to Joan that we are most apt to describe the behavior as autonomous. As we shall see in a few pages, this is so because such unique assessments are more clearly assessments which reflect the presence of the agent in question. To the extent that *any* agent must make the same assessment, the account of why the agent behaved as she did does not rest upon the particular agent in question, but seems more reflective of the circumstances or influences which are present. As we shall see in greater detail below, this is why we do not hold coerced behavior, which plays upon values no sensible agent would risk, to be autonomous action.

The formal conception of autonomy as autarkeia cannot account for this intuition. In fact, the principle of universalization would seem to indicate it is precisely behaviors which are not unique to *this agent* which are autonomous: autonomous action would not be peculiar to some contingent, empirical fact (like the presence of a particular agent). But it is precisely behavior which **is** unique to this agent, *which reflects this agent's judgement*, that we most wish to describe as autonomous.

This is especially true if we are concerned to develop a concept of autonomy which can serve as a basis for moral responsibility. We ascribe responsibility to an agent for the production of some result if we believe it was the presence of that agent which accounts for the result in question. To ascribe responsibility, we look for the contribution which the agent made to the production of the result, and this contribution is the active assessment of various influences, by which the agent directed his behavior one way rather than another. This is why we require self control for the ascription of responsibility. It is the presumption of self control which allows us to account for behavior through the agent, rather than some other force. By assessing the various influences, the agent contributes the *direction* of action, and controls whether *this* behavior or *that* behavior will be performed.

The substantive notion of autonomy I have offered, which focuses upon the agent's active assessment of external influences, reflects a view of autonomous *action* as action which reflects the active judgement of the agent in question (regardless of how that agent came to be as she is). The focus upon active assessment by the agent, and the contribution this makes to the account of why the agent behaved as she did, offers a model for describing autonomous action and distinguishing such action from non-autonomous behavior. This distinction rests upon the contribution the agent makes to the determination of action, and our recognition that it is the contribution the agent makes that identifies autonomy. Let us return to Aristotle's metaphor of the helmsman to make this distinction.

Compulsion

A ruler is as the helmsman of a ship, and steers according to practical wisdom. However, certain external influences (such as an extremely strong current, or violent storm) may at times threaten the helmsman's ability to steer his own course. When this happens, the agent's autonomy is threatened.

Thus, external influences must not act as helmsman. So long as these influences do not steer behavior, but merely influence how the agent steers (by effecting the "mean" as currents or weather would normally effect a ship's helmsman), they pose no threat to one's ability to rule one's own life. The issue is one of who is helmsman: the agent, or the external influences? In keeping with the analogy of the helmsman, Aristotle describes compulsion as follows:

> ...that is compulsory of which the moving principle is outside, being a principle in which nothing is **contributed** by the person who is acting or is feeling the passion, e.g. *if he were to be carried somewhere by wind*...(EN 1110a1-5; emphasis added).

The answer to the question of who acts as helmsman lacks a sharp line of distinction. In reality our actions, with the exception of actions which are physically forced (such as my arm being pushed into someone else), all contain elements of both circumstantial influences and the agent's evaluative assessment. Although the notion of autonomy as self-rule does not generally view external influences as compulsory, there are some influences which surely threaten the agent's role as helmsman. Aristotle recognizes some situations to be in some sense threatening to an agent's control when he states:

> But with regard to the things that are done from fear of greater evils or for some noble object (e.g. if a tyrant were to order one to do something base, having one's parents and children in his power, and if one did the action they were to be saved, but otherwise would be put to death), it may be debated whether such actions are involuntary or voluntary. Something of the sort happens also with regard to the throwing of goods overboard in a storm; for in the abstract no one throws goods away voluntarily, but on condition of securing the safety of himself and his crew any sensible man does so.(EN 111oa5-10)

In this discussion, Aristotle recognizes such actions as "mixed": they are voluntary, but the determination of action does not reflect the agent's practical wisdom so much as it does the circumstances at hand. Because *any* sensible agent must choose this behavior, there is no unique contribution which the particular agent in question adds through her assessment of these influences. The agent here cannot be said to act as helmsman.

We can begin to see here the emergence of a standard to distinguish action which an agent steers from that which he does not. The standard invokes the idea of a "sensible man", and is alluded to in the above passage when Aristotle states that to throw goods overboard during a storm to save himself and his crew is something that "any sensible man" would do. The standard is invoked again when Aristotle discusses actions done in circumstances which "overstrain" human nature:

> On some actions praise indeed is not bestowed, but pardon is, when one does what he ought not under pressure which overstrains human nature and which no one could withstand.(EN 1110a25)

The fact that Aristotle recognizes that such action results from pressure which "overstrains human nature" indicates that he views such disproportionate options as in some sense eliminating the agent as helmsman, as weather might overstrain a ship's helmsman (so that the ship is "carried away by wind"). The metaphor of the helmsman, then, rests upon the assumption that when the direction of behavior reflects the unique evaluative assessment of the agent in question, the agent acts as helmsman. When **no** sensible agent could have done otherwise, we do not account for the direction of the behavior by reference to some quality or characteristic of the evaluative assessment of the agent in question, and so the agent does not act as helmsman.

This standard can help us to understand not only the threat posed to autonomy by the types of compulsive circumstances described above, but can also help us to distinguish autonomous action from coerced behavior. Let us look at this in more detail.

Coercion

Coercion poses a special problem to autonomy, because it operates through the agent's own evaluative assessments. Coercion plays upon the agent's assessment of some option as important in order to steer the agent: it is because the agent so values one option that *she brings herself* to act in a particular way. For example, it is because an agent values her life that the threat to kill her will steer her to act in a particular way. If the agent doesn't care if she lives or dies, the threat loses its coercive force.

Let us look at what would be taken as a paradigmatic case of coercion. I put a gun to your head and order you to walk across the street. It may be argued that you have the option to be shot in the head, but none of us considers this a viable option in this circumstance. What is it that bothers us about acknowledging the option of being shot in the head as a viable option? Is it that we are faced with harm? I do not think so, for just as Aristotle recognized that 'mixed' action could result from "evils or from some noble object"(EN 1110a5), we can change the situation so that the offer is of a pleasant nature, rather than a threat to life. For example, "If you wish to receive a Ph.D., walk across the street", when we have no real desire not to walk across the street. Again, it seems there is a compulsive nature to our walking across the street, even though we have the option to remain where we are (and thus not receive the Ph.D).

What we find coercive about the situations is the relative desirability of the options with which we are presented. The weight of our "aim" to stay alive far exceeds the weight of our "aim" to not do something as trivial as walk across the street, and **no** "sensible man" could choose otherwise. Likewise, the weight of our desire to receive the Ph.D. is so disproportionate to our desire to stand still, that we walk across the street. The severe disproportionality of options seems to pre-empt "steering" by the agent, by so weighting one option that all other options are relatively weightless. because **no** sensible man could choose otherwise, the agent in question seems to add no contribution through her own evaluative assessment.

We can see, then, why the order, "walk across the street if you want the Ph.D. that you've worked so many years to get" may be compulsive ("He had no choice..."), while the order, "kill twelve innocent people if you want the Ph.D." is not ("He should not have done it..."). In the former case, the situation is manipulated so that the available options are extremely disproportionate; so much so that no "sensible man" could choose to do otherwise. In the latter case, to avoid the death of twelve innocent people is at least as strong, if not more so, an end as receiving a Ph.D.! This seems to be what Aristotle had in mind when he stated:

> But some acts, perhaps, we cannot be forced to do, but ought rather to face death after the most fearful sufferings; for the things that 'forced' Euripides' Alcmaeon to slay his mother seem absurd.(EN 1110a25-27)

This standard of disproportionality is an abstract standard to be sure. As Aristotle states, "It is difficult sometimes to determine what should be chosen at what cost, and what should be endured in return for what gain..." (EN 1110a27-30). Nonetheless, a standard does exist: Does the behavior reflect the agent's evaluative assessment, or are the circumstances such that no sensible man could choose otherwise, and thus the determination of action reflects the circumstances more than the agent's evaluative assessment? If it is the latter, the ship's course reflects more the external circumstances than the agent's practical wisdom. If it is the former, the agent acts as helmsman.

The Sensible Man

Why should the sensible man standard be important to the concept of autonomy? It would seem quite possible, for example, for a man to decide **not** to throw goods overboard in a storm to save himself and his crew (as described in the earlier example). Would not this man be considered autonomous?

For Aristotle, the helmsman steers according to practical wisdom (in the form of the "mean"). This requires that he not allow desire, for example, to "steer one to indulge in every pleasure". When one's action does not fall within the boundaries of excess and deficiency, one seems not to steer one's own behavior (it is desire, for example, which steers one to indulge in every pleasure).

Aristotle's description of the mean is concerned with virtuous action. We are not concerned here with virtue, as Aristotle is. However, we **do** share Aristotle's concern that helmsmanship reflect a form of practical wisdom (though it need not be "virtuous"). Thus, we share with Aristotle a concern to identify boundaries to when an agent's determination of action reflects her own practical assessments.

These boundaries are set by the actual state of the world, and whether the agent is steering in this context. To steer *actual* behavior in the *actual* world, one must have a reasonably accurate conception of the conditions of the world which serve as the context within which she steers. This is not to require *absolute* accuracy, for none of us would meet this condition. Rather, it is to require a "reasonably" accurate conception of the world; one which displays an ability to recognize one's circumstances, and appreciate them. We may debate exactly how much accuracy it is reasonable to require. But surely *some* degree of accuracy **is** required.

Susan Wolf also recognizes this requirement, that an agent have a reasonably accurate conception of the world, as a condition of self-control.[6] Wolf argues that while responsibility does not require *ultimate* control over one's "deepest self", it does require "sanity". Wolf describes sanity as follows:

> We may understand sanity, then, as the minimally sufficient ability cognitively and normatively to recognize and appreciate the world for what it is...[7]

The requirement of sanity is not a requirement that an agent's action merely be determined by her practical assessments. Rather, it is a requirement that these practical assessments which determine behavior be related to the world in an appropriate way:

> Some insane people...may have complete control of their actions, and even complete control of their acting selves. The desire to be sane is thus not a desire for another form of control; it is rather a desire that one's self be connected to the world in a certain way...[8]

Wolf goes on to tell us that the way one's self is connected to the world which constitutes sanity is through an "accurate conception of the world".[9] This accurate conception involves the ability to recognize and appreciate certain fundamental values and actual states of the world. The "sensible man" must be sane in this way.

Additionally, human nature sets certain boundaries on autonomous reasoning.[10] To have an appreciation of the world as it is involves an appreciation of the type of creatures we are. The types of creatures we are place boundaries upon the types of assessments we might "reasonably" make. This, however, does not threaten the ability of agents to make unique assessments. This boundary does not require conformity. It does require a certain *structure* of reasoning. For example, we understand humans as the types of creatures who might place great value on religious belief. To choose an action which will result in death on religious grounds, then, would be understandable in structure. This is true even if the particular religious beliefs in question are quite unpopular, or **unique** to the agent in question. The action is "reasonable" because it is "sane", and is consistent with the *type* of reasons we understand human beings as acting for.

Conversely, imagine a person who, without any medical, psychological, or other apparent reason for undertaking the project, decided that she would take steps to place herself in a permanently vegetative state on the basis of a passing urge. The adoption of such a project lacks an appreciation of the type of creatures human beings are. We do not understand human beings as the types of creatures who assess passing urges as greater than the permanent damage of being placed in the vegetative state described above. One of the identifying features of "reasonable" humans is the ability to forego such activity in the interests of long-term survival. When such passing urges are acted upon to the detriment of long-term survival, and there are no "understandable" reasons present, we describe the person as "compelled" by the urge; we do not consider them autonomous. In this way, human nature itself places boundaries upon "sensible" assessments.

To return, then, to the man who chooses to die rather than throw goods overboard in a storm to save himself and his crew: on the face of it, his behavior does not appear autonomous. He seems to assess the loss of the goods **and** himself and his crew as the option to take over the loss of the goods only. Unless there are additional considerations which would make his behavior more consistent with the actual features of his circumstances and human nature itself, he seems not to act appropriately "sensible". The inappropriateness of his assessment does not stem from a disagreement about what should be assessed in what way; for example, it is not a disagreement about what prudential rationality calls for. Rather, the inappropriateness of the assessment stems from its apparent lack of appreciation of the agent's circumstances, options, and of human nature itself.

The sensible man standard is vital for defining the boundaries of autonomy. While there may exist disagreement with my particular articulation of the standards of "sensibility" in terms of "sanity" and "human nature", that some such standard is vital is beyond question. Without this standard, *any* action based upon a first-person assessment must be considered autonomous; compelling circumstances or coercion become meaningless concepts. But we simply do not conceive of autonomy in this way. We do not consider many actions which meet the requirement of first-person assessment to be autonomous. For example, compulsion, coercion, behavior based upon (insane) paranoid delusions, or even behavior under the influence of a drug are not considered autonomous.[11] Autonomy requires more than mere agency. Autonomy involves a notion of reasonable sanity and competence.

An Adequate Range of Options

The standard used to evaluate autonomy as described above offers a glimpse at the features which autonomous behavior displays. Thus far, we have described autonomy in terms of behavior which is accounted for by the presence of a particular agent in given circumstances. It is *that agent's* assessment of a set of circumstances and influences which steers behavior. Autonomy thus requires that the agent's assessment play a key role in the determination of action. For this to be so, an agent must have a range of options to assess, and available options whose assessment is not pre-determined for a sensible agent (a sensible agent might assess things otherwise).

If an agent does not have an adequate range of viable options, the determination of behavior cannot be a reflection of the agent's active evaluative assessment. This requirement of an adequate range of options is held by many current autonomy theorists. For example, it is central to the conception of autonomy advanced by Joseph Raz.[12] Now, we can see clearly the conceptual basis of this requirement: if the agent's assessment is to account for the determination of action, a "sensible" agent must have a range of viable options to choose from.

When an adequate range of options is available, it is the presence of the agent which accounts for a particular behavior. This is true even if the vast majority of people, or even *everyone*, chooses the same option. It is not that *only this agent* would choose a particular option which points the account of behavior toward the agent. What points the account toward the agent is that *this behavior* was chosen by the agent, when a variety of viable options were available.

While assessments which are unique to a particular agent are (if sane) more apt to be described as autonomous, this is because they are more clearly not compelled or coerced (and so more clearly deserving of an ascription of autonomy). What makes us so apt to ascribe autonomy to these assessments is simply that, if sane, assessments which are unique to some agent are clearly not assessments which *any* sensible agent must make.

On this view, even assessments which *every* agent does in practice make might be autonomous, for they may not be assessments which every sensible agent *must* make. In order for it to be the case that every sensible agent *must* make some assessment, in must be the case that to assess things otherwise would be to lack a recognition of, and appreciation for, the world as it actually is and human nature itself (as described in our earlier discussion of the sensible man). When no man could choose otherwise and remain sensible in this manner, autonomy does not apply. And when no viable options are available, a *sensible* man could not choose otherwise. Thus, the presence of an adequate range of options is a vital condition for autonomy.

Conclusion

In developing the helmsman metaphor, we have identified a variety of features and conditions of autonomy. First, autonomy is concerned that the account for why a particular behavior is taken be centered around *the agent's* contribution to the determination of behavior. This consists of accounting for behavior through the agent's assessment of various options. This assessment, however, is not an unqualified condition of autonomy. Autonomy consists of more than mere agency. Autonomy consists of agency exercised under certain conditions of "sanity", and free of compulsive or coercive influences. These influences are identified through the ability of a "sensible" agent to choose otherwise. And this ability to choose otherwise requires the presence of an adequate range of viable options. When these conditions and features are present, the agent acts as "helmsman" in the determination of her behavior. We thus ascribe autonomy to behavior determined under these conditions and features.

[1] Gibbard, Alan Wise Choices, Apt Feelings (Cambridge: Harvard University Press, 1990), p.18.

[2] Gibbard, Wise Choices, Apt Feelings, p.18.

[3] Gibbard, Wise Choices, Apt Feelings, p.19.

[4] For example, see E.J. Bond's distinction between "Motivating Reasons" and "Grounding Reasons" in Reason and Value (New York: Cambridge University Press, 1982); and Joseph Raz's distinction between "Explanatory Reasons" and "Guiding Reasons" in Practical Reason and Norms (Princeton: Princeton University Press, 1990).

[5] See discussion of Dworkin in chapter one.

[6] Wolf, Susan "Sanity and the Metaphysics of Responsibility" in Schoeman, Ferdinand (ed.), Responsibility, Character and the Emotions (New York: Cambridge University Press, 1987), pp.46-62.

[7] Wolf, "Sanity and the Metaphysics of Responsibility", p.56.

[8] Wolf, "Sanity and the Metaphysics of Responsibility", p.55.

[9] Wolf, "Sanity and the Metaphysics of Responsibility", p.55.

[10] This idea developed from a seminar on "value" offered by R.G. Frey. I would like to thank Professor Frey and the members of that seminar for stimulating these ideas.

[11] We may, however, find the agent responsible for autonomously placing themselves in this condition. For example, the captain of the Exxon Valdez is held responsible for being in a drunken condition. But this is different than finding the actual behavior under this condition to be autonomous.

[12] See Raz, Joseph The Morality of Freedom.

CHAPTER FOUR:
Addressing Kant's Concerns

In the second chapter we saw that Immanuel Kant attempted to build the concept of autonomy upon a conception of self-sufficiency, in order to achieve self-determination which was not diluted by the influence of external considerations. I argued that self-sufficiency was too rigorous to serve as a basis for a useful concept of autonomy, and in the second half of that chapter offered a model of autonomy based upon the metaphor of the helmsman, which can help us to understand autonomy in modern society. In chapter three I discussed how we are to understand autonomy in the context of external influences, distinguishing compulsive and coercive influences from influences which do not threaten individual autonomy.

However, we have not yet addressed the concerns which led Kant to formulate autonomy in terms of self-sufficiency. As we saw in chapter two, Kant believed that external considerations made the moral value of action dependent upon the contingent presence or absence of those considerations. This attaches moral value to the action in the context of external considerations, and allows those considerations, rather than reason, to guide moral determinations (or, at a motivational level, action). For example, if desires were allowed to influence the will, the will would be guided by reference to the object or state of affairs which one desired, rather than being self-directing.

The problem here is that for Kant, to base the will on desire is to will the object or state of affairs which I desire as my effect. To do this is to conceive of myself as a means,[1] and to ascribe the determination of my will to the object or state of affairs desired.[2] For example, if I value pleasure and allow the consideration of how much pleasure would result from each of a variety of potential actions to influence my determination of action (perhaps determining action according to which action would result in the most pleasure), it seems the amount of pleasure an action would result in (which is beyond my control) is what guides my behavior.

To understand Kant's fears here, we must remember his historical roots, and his wish to avoid the conclusions of David Hume: that reason is, and ought to be, slave to the passions. Kant held that reason is the highest function of man, and that nature is such that man should be directed by this characteristic, rather than desire.[3] To propose that reason is slave to the passions, and that man simply determines the appropriate means to the ends established by the object of desire (or any other external consideration, for that matter), is to endanger the view of man as a free being, to view man as a mere "cog" in a mechanistic world, and thus fail to appreciate the proper role of reason and the dignity of man.

These concerns are profound, and indeed it would seem that to view man as directed by the objects of desire in such a way as to relegate reason to the role of slave to the passions is to threaten a viable concept of autonomy. However, I will argue below that the Humean view, that desire-based motivation relegates human judgement to the role of slave to the passions, is misguided. Indeed, to adequately understand motivation, we must posit human judgement in the role of "helmsman" within the context of multiple desires and other influences.

In establishing this, we shall not accomplish fully Kant's goal of establishing the action as an end in itself. We are still, to some extent, subject to his criticism that our actions are conceived as a means to the production of the state of affairs desired. But we do avoid the feature that such action is determined by the object of desire in such a way that we fall into a Humean view that man's judgement is slave to desire. We do not ascribe the determination of our action to the object or state of affairs desired, but to our own assessment of desires and other influences.

By positing man's judgement as helmsman, we understand the action as a means to an end whose direction is set by the agent herself. While this direction is set in light of considerations many of which are beyond the agent's control, the direction itself is not simply a product of these factual considerations, but a product of the agent's active assessment of factual information. This is all we require for a plausible conception of autonomy. Let us look at this more closely.

Desires and Motivation

The "Humean" theory of motivation[4] takes motivated action to be the product of reason and desire. Desire by itself cannot result in action without the determination of appropriate means to satisfy the desire; Likewise, the determination of appropriate means to some end will not result in action unless that end is desired. On this model, it is desire which plays the role of motivational force.

In more recent discussions of motivation, this "Humean" model has evolved into what is today known as the "Desire-Belief" model of motivation.[5] To be moved to action X, I must have a desire for end Y and a belief that action X is the appropriate means for achieving this end. As the only role for the agent's evaluative capacities in this model is to determine the appropriate means to achieve an end established by desire, the agent's evaluative capacities seem passive in that the agent's assessments are a reaction to the end established by desire and the set of beliefs the agent holds.

However, the view that external influences dictate behavior is inadequate. After all, we must ask the question of what it means to say that one influence is stronger than another. For example, if desire is the motive force behind human action, and we recognize more than one desire may be present at any given moment, motivation hinges upon the assessment we make of <u>which desire shall motivate</u>.

The model of motivation in which action results from the strongest present desire neglects to account for how 'strength of desire' is assessed. Not all desires are felt passions, and it is certainly not the case that an uncontested desire will necessarily result in action. Abstinence and sacrifice are common exceptions to simple desire-based motivation which seem to indicate an ability on the part of an agent to make assessments of various desires. For example, imagine a man who desires to eat. However, because of certain values he attaches to religious convictions, he takes an oath to fast. In doing so he chooses to assess the desire to eat in such a way that he will not act upon it.

At other times, however, it seems that desires might override the agent's own evaluative assessments. The example of the person who might act on a passing urge to place themselves in a permanently vegetative state, which I discussed in the previous chapter, is one instance. This would surely threaten autonomy, as desire in these cases would seem to relegate a person's evaluative capacities to a subservient role. I will argue that these cases are rare indeed, and that most cases in which we loosely describe desires as "compelling action" are not accurately described in these terms. The types of boundaries established by "sanity" and the "sensible person" standards outlined in the previous chapter are quite broad, and leave significant room for the agent's own evaluative assessments to lead to unique determinations. Indeed, as we shall discuss below, most cases described as weakness of will are not instances of an agent's lack of control over the assessment of behavior at all.

What we are describing is an evaluation that the subject *should have*, or would *liked to have*, evaluated present desires differently. And this may pose real problems to Freedom of the Will. But as we have seen, being able to will what one wants to will is a different question than whether one acts as one wills (however that will is determined). That our actions result from our own assessments of various desires (and other influences) seems in most cases beyond question, even if we wish we assessed things differently.

It may be argued that there remains a question about the formation of the agent's will: The agent directs behavior according to her active assessment of various influences, but the assessment the agent makes may not itself be under the control of the agent. But this is to raise a different question, one about freedom of the will, and not about the agent's control over her behavior. Indeed, it may seem at an intuitive level these questions are intertwined, but in reality they are not. We are concerned here with an agent's control of her action: we are concerned to show that an agent can be said to direct her own behavior in the context of external influences. In this, we are maintaining that the agent's behavior is determined by her will, however that will itself is formed.

Freedom of Will vs. Freedom of Action

We are concerned with freedom of action, not freedom of will. If we do not recognize this distinction, we shall be unable to develop a plausible account of moral responsibility *for action*; and it is *action* we are concerned with here. We ascribe to agents autonomy and moral responsibility based upon their behavior; we do so, in Kant's words, *as if* their will were also free. The latter question we may never know the answer to. The former is the level at which we understand our world.

Gerald Dworkin's confusion concerning autonomy and identification stems from his preoccupation with an agent's will.[6] Thus, Dworkin wishes to tie autonomy to freedom of the will, and so describes autonomous action as those actions which reflect a will we have freely chosen. But as I indicated earlier, autonomy should be tied to freedom of action. After all, what we are concerned with within the concept of autonomy is identifying certain *actions* as those of the agent in question.

Traditionally, questions concerning the relationship between an agent and her behavior have oscillated between the issues of "freedom of the will" and "freedom of action", often appearing to lack appreciation of this distinction. In this, "free action" and "free will" have been supposed to be, if not identical, at least interdependent. But the separation of these issues is greater than is often recognized. While both are, to be sure, concerned with freedom, each issue takes up the question of freedom at a different level. Where freedom of action is concerned with an agent's ability to act as he wishes, freedom of will is concerned with the agent's ability to in some sense be as he wishes.

Broadly speaking, freedom of the will is the ability to will what we want to will. It is present when our will is not "determined", or in some sense necessitated to be as it is. Thus, the control that is important for freedom of the will is the control over what our will is; are we free to have the will we wish to have, or is what our will is beyond our control?

This contrasts to the control that is important for freedom of action. Freedom of action is concerned with the control a person has over his behavior. Is the agent able to act as he wills, or is the agent's behavior brought about by some other force? The question of freedom of action is concerned with distinguishing action which results from an agent's will, whether or not that will is as it is because the agent has chosen it, from action which does not.

It is easy to see here why these two notions are easily conflated. At first glance, it seems that if a person's will is brought about by some other force, the action which results from that will is not within the agent's control. Thus, several attempts have been made to give the agent some degree of control over his will through the ability to revise his will[7], or to re-order his will[8], but these attempts seem futile. As Susan Wolf has pointed out,

> ...no matter how many levels of self we posit, there will still, in any individual case, be a last level - a deepest self about whom the question "What governs it?" will arise, problematic as ever.[9]

It seems there must be some level at which we must admit we have no control. We just are as we are. While we may thus lack control over being this way, we still can distinguish actions which result from our being this way from actions which do not. Why must we insist on control at an existential level?

While I am sure that I will make few converts on this issue here, the query itself demonstrates the separation of the question of 'freedom of action' from the question of 'freedom of the will'. It is at least possible to maintain that an agent's action is under the control of the agent's will, but that the agent's will is not under the agent's control. The question of autonomy is the question of determining one's own action oneself, however that self is determined.

If we do not recognize this distinction when we attempt to ascribe responsibility, we are faced with a.) allowing that to some extent no one is responsible for behavior; b.) that no influence (other that sheer physical force) is a threat to responsibility; or c.) an infinite regress. For example, if we approach responsibility through the issue of freedom of the will and assume determinism, no one is responsible for any action. If we assume free will, we are faced with the prospect of saying that the person who performs an action under threat of death is responsible, because she could have chosen to die. To assume neither determinism nor free will but require a "test" for free will (allowing that the will may sometimes be free and sometimes not, or in some senses free and in some senses not) will lead to the infinite regress described by Susan Wolf above. None of these options are plausible. To approach responsibility for action through freedom of the will is misguided. We must approach responsibility through the question of freedom of action.

Motivation vs. Causation

Having established that here we are concerned with the agent's ability to determine (through the agent's assessments) what *action* to take, and not how the assessment itself is grounded (in terms of how an agent comes to **be** as she is), let us return to the question of the practical efficacy of an agent's assessments in determining action. Can the agent's assessment steer the determination of action, or is action the result of some "causal" mechanism of desire and circumstance (as Kant feared)?

Imagine once again a man who has a desire to eat. On the other hand, he acknowledges that he values being thin and healthy. Yet, the man eats. Does the desire to eat compel the man to eat, or simply provide the man with a reason to eat which he then may choose to act upon or not to act upon, and which wins out in competition with his desire to be thin. Surely it is the latter.

I acknowledge that people often, indeed usually, act in order to satisfy some desire. But I maintain that they act in this way because they value (or at least do not disvalue) the satisfaction of the desire. The value the man in the above example attaches to the satisfaction of his desire to eat is compared to the value he attaches to being thin, and satisfying his hunger is assessed as the reason to act upon. Indeed, people often attach great value to the immediate elimination of hunger, often much greater than they would like. But this does not mean that we *must* act for this reason.

We must be careful not to conflate *motivation* and *causation*. The "Desire-Belief" model is often taken as a causal model of motivation: The desires I have *cause* me to act in a particular way (given that I have a particular set of beliefs). Perhaps the best known modern proponent of such a view is Donald Davidson. The following passage from the introduction of his book Essays on Actions and Events illustrates such an outlook:

> "Actions, Reasons, and Causes" was a reaction against a widely accepted doctrine that the explanation of an intentional action in terms of motives or reasons could not relate reasons and actions as cause and effect.[10]

Davidson's work has been very influential in encouraging the understanding of motivation in terms of causation. However, this understanding is flawed. The trouble with such a view is that it is misleading in its characterization of the way in which external considerations influence actions. By describing motivation in causal terms, there is a tendency to conflate motivation and scientific causation.[11] This conflation encourages a view of motivation which involves a compulsory connection between external considerations and motivation which is only mitigated by what beliefs I hold; Given that I have a particular set of beliefs, a desire X will result in action Y. Hence the belief that external influences "dictate" action.

However, there is a significant difference between scientific causation and motivation. Davidson himself recognizes substantial differences in the way "causation" is to be understood in terms of actions and the way "causation" is understood in science.[12] This difference is not trivial; what "causation" means for each usage is a different **type** of thing, rather than different tokens of the same type of phenomenon. This distinction can be traced to Plato, who discussed two different kinds of causes in the Timaeus (46c-48a) and the Laws (X 894d-898c). One kind of cause refers to those causes "which, being moved by others, are compelled to move others". The second kind of cause involves those causes "which are endowed with mind and are the workers of things good and fair". Examples of each are given by Plato in the Phaedo (98c-99b):

> a.) The reason why I am lying here now is that my body is composed of bones and sinews, and since the bones move freely in their joints the sinews by relaxing and contracting enable me somehow to bend my limbs, and that is the cause of my sitting here in a bent position.

> b.) Since Athens has thought it better to condemn me, therefore I for my part have thought it better to sit here, and more right to stay and submit to whatever penalty she orders.

The first example uses the term 'cause' in a way which involves a necessary connection. This causation is chain-like, and the connection between that which causes movement and movement is compulsory. By contrast, in the second example there is no necessary connection between that which motivates and action, and no consideration need necessarily motivate. The agent assesses what considerations should be acted upon. Here, motivational force is provided by the agent rather than transferred from a "cause". Desires, circumstances, etc. may or may not affect motivation; External considerations are simply facts which provide <u>potential</u> ends for the agent, rather than compulsory "causes" of action. The agent assesses which considerations should prevail.

However, some would argue that an agent cannot assess desires in this way. Hume himself thought desire to be immune to critical evaluation. Let us consider this viewpoint then, in the context of the strongest apparent example of an agent's inability to control effective motivation: Those cases of akrasia, or weakness of will.

Akrasia

The classical conception of weakness of will pits the agent's will against desire, or immediate passion. For Aristotle[13], there seem to be two conflicting syllogisms, one of desire and one of "reason". When the syllogism of desire wins out, thus keeping the agent from acting on his judgement of what is best, we have a case of weakness of will. Aquinas[14] also characterizes Akrasia as a battle between reason and desire. Aquinas believes that passion hinders the agent's ability to do as he should. Thus, weakness of will results from the agent acting on passion rather than his best judgement. What the classical accounts of akrasia seem to share is a characterization of akrasia in terms of a conflict between desire and the agent's "better judgement". In acting on desire rather than his "better judgement", the agent displays weakness of will.[15]

It would be wise here to heed the warning of J.L. Austin, who complains that we often "...collapse succumbing to temptation into losing control of ourselves...".[16] When we ask whether motivation is subject to cognitive assessment, we should not "beg the question" by requiring that any such assessment have an outcome of a particular type. It is this mistake that I feel is made in most traditional examples of weakness of will. By pitting desire against "better judgement", and defining weakness of will as those cases in which desire wins out, we seem unable to make assessments of desire-based motivations as preferable to these "better standards". It is this which Gary Watson seems to have in mind when he states,

> ...'what one most wants' may mean either the object of the strongest desire or what one most values...The problem of free action arises because what one desires may not be what one values, and what one most values may not be what one is finally moved to get."[17]

An agent's will, for Watson, is determined by a variety of reasons for action, an evaluation of one's desire-based motivations <u>and</u> one's value-based motivations. Free action, for Watson, is simply action which is the result of this evaluational judgement, which does not ignore the presence of desires we may wish we did not have.

Let us keep in mind the shift we have made away from autarkeia toward self-rule. We must not require that all (potential) motives be present in an autarkic fashion. While we may wish that we did not have certain desires (much as a ship's helmsman may wish the waters were not rough), autonomy as self-rule requires that we acknowledge the presence of these desires in determining action if we are to act as helmsman. The view of autonomy as self-rule does not require that we have only those motives we wish to have, but requires only that our behavior reflect our own assessment of those (potential) motives we <u>do</u> have.

This is important, for it is often the case that people regret their decisions, indeed often as they are making them. For example, I may watch the baseball game instead of read one evening, knowing that such a decision is not the one that I should make. But this regret surely does not mean I lack control over my actions.

Let us examine some examples of weakness of will. In a recent essay[18], Thomas Hill offers five ways in which weakness of will is thought to be manifested in human behavior. We shall examine each in turn, and demonstrate that each would be more appropriately characterized as a problem of freedom of will, rather than a problem of weakness of will. In each of the cases Hill describes, we can understand the types of reasons for which the person acts (the assessments fall within the boundaries set by "sanity" and the "sensible person" standards outlined in the previous chapter), but the agent *appears* to be unable to act on her assessments because she wishes her action were based upon considerations other than those for which she acts. However, I will argue that in each case Hill describes, it is perfectly consistent to say that the agent acted on the basis of her assessment (demonstrates freedom of action), but wishes that she assessed things differently (does not demonstrate freedom of will). Hill describes each manifestation of weakness of will in the behavior of Amy:

> (I) *Half-hearted efforts.* She often takes part in challenging activities, such as competitive sports and arguing with her opinionated husband, but she rarely tries very hard. She wants to win and makes some feeble efforts in that direction, but when the challenge becomes difficult she never exerts herself fully. She does not exactly "give up", for she continues to take minimal steps towards winning, hoping that somehow they will be enough. Usually she does not explicitly resolve to win, or even to try hard, but she undertakes the activities with winning as the end in view and she carries on without ever deciding to abandon the end. People say that she has the ability but not the strength of will to win. The problem is not simply a particular aversion to success in competition; she behaves in a similar way whenever her projects become difficult.[19]

In the above case, Amy's weakness of will is manifested in her not putting forth the appropriate effort. But this seems to be a case where Amy simply wills leisure and laziness more than she wills to win. Perhaps she would not like to will leisure and laziness so greatly, but then *that* is a problem wherein Amy is not able to will what she wants to will

- a problem of freedom of will, not weakness of will.

> (2) *Weak Resolves.* Sometimes she deliberates and makes resolutions about her future conduct. Each year, for example, she makes a list of New Year's resolutions about dieting, jogging, reading good books, etc. But often the resolutions are half-hearted even when they are made. She says, quite sincerely, that she intends to keep them, and by announcing them she puts herself in the position of being embarrassed and a bit ashamed if she does not. But she would not be surprised if later she "changed her mind", and she purposefully vague about what she would count as a good reason for changing her mind. She makes charts for daily reminders and feels good about the "new direction" she is giving her life; but she knows that she could be persuaded to deviate even at that moment if the right opportunity came along. These resolves do not usually last long, sometimes giving way to considerations that seem more important at the time and sometimes simply fading into insignificant memories.[20]

Again, it would seem that Amy simply wills what she resolves less than she wills other things. Hill states that "these resolves...sometimes give way to considerations that seem more important at the time...". It would seem that Amy simply does not will her resolves as much as she should, or would like to. But again, this is a case concerned with how Amy's will should be, not a case concerned with the connection of her will to behavior. Thus, this case would more appropriately be characterized as a problem of freedom of will, not weakness of will.

> (3) *Surrendering after a struggle.* At times, however, Amy makes more whole-hearted commitments. As she anticipates certain future situations, it is extremely important to her that she respond in one way rather than another...She is keenly aware of the temptations and pres-

sures that will incline her to respond in the least preferred way; and in anticipation of this, she makes a solemn and explicit resolution forbidding her to "change her mind" for such reasons....But, as time passes and the anticipated temptations arise, she "feels torn" between her resolution and her immediate wants. When she reflects on her earlier perspective, she wants to carry out her resolution and she is angry that she hesitates; but when she focuses upon the situation at hand, she prefers to do something else and is annoyed that she ever made the resolution. In these situations typically she chooses to break the resolution, knowing full well her reason for doing so but soon feeling regrets and "kicking herself" for changing her mind in the very sort of situation she planned and "told herself" not to.[21]

This case seems close to the classical conception of weakness of will. Upon reflection, Amy wishes to do X, but immediate desire pushes her to act against this "reflective judgement". But, as was the case when we discussed the classical conception, why are immediate wants not considered part of an agent's will? Perhaps we feel we should not be so "superficial", but then this would be a case where we wished our will were different (we wish our will weren't so strongly affected by immediate wants). It seems that the struggle is internal to the will; what shall Amy will to do? Although she may wish that the struggle turned out differently (and thus that her will were different), that is a problem of freedom of will, not weakness of will.

> (4) *Fading Will.* Sometimes she resolves to do something, but then her will seems simply to fade away. Though she may be determined and quite explicit at the outset, as time goes on she thinks less about her plan and when she does, it seems less important. It is not that she literally "forgets" her resolve when she deviates from it, thinking when she remembers, "Oh, yes, I planned not to

do that." Nor does she reconsider in the light of a new situation and alter the plan. She does not lose an inner battle, or simply find herself, much to her surprise, acting contrary to what she now concludes she should do. She may have no opinion about which is best, the old plan or the current choice. It is as if she hears but does not bother to listen to the plans and orders she earlier left for herself.[22]

This case seems to be a case wherein we should question whether Amy has a will at all. If her resolves are paid no attention, in what sense could they be said to represent what she wills? Let us remember here that weakness of will is *intentionally* doing what the agent knows to be contrary to her will. If a fading will is a will which is paid no attention, in what sense can it be said to be her will? It would seem more analogous to information one knows about but does not care about. In this case, Amy knows that she resolved to do X, but seems to lack a will to carry out her resolves. While she may experience "weakness of resolves", she does not experience "weakness of will". Why should a will be required to attach to resolves when they are present?

(5) *Unstable will.* Earlier, when she was less reflective, Amy did not make explicit resolutions but was more prepared to exert herself fully in the project of the day. The trouble was that she kept changing her projects. One day she was "determined" to be a musician; but the next day she was enthusiastic about being an athlete; another time, she decided to be a great surgeon. Each time she worked hard at the project, bought instruments, running shoes, dissecting kit, etc., and gave up parties to study and practice; but, lacking a good sense of the sacrifices requires, she never anticipated the temptations to give up and so never made any explicit resolutions to overcome them. For a while she had a will to do each of these things; but it was a fragile and unstable will, easily "broken" by pa-

rental ridicule and readily changed when new role models captured her imagination.[23]

In this final case, it seems weakness of will is connected to a lack of any stable, long-term "lifeplan". Amy's will is constantly changing; she is unable to stick to any consistent plan. Perhaps we would like to have a stable will, but why should such stability be *required*? The fact that our will is unstable only indicates that our will is not as we would like it to be, rather than indicating that we are experiencing a "weakness of will".

All of the above cases embody what Austin warns us against: collapsing succumbing to temptation with weakness of will. The will is thought of in some ideal form - either stable, attached to resolutions, or free of immediate desire. When the agent's behavior does not reflect this ideal will, it is thought that his will is weak. However, why should we believe a will must reflect such ideal forms if it is not to be weak? While it may be true that our will is not as we wish it were, it surely does not follow that our will is *weak*.

Recent discussions of overcoming akrasia point to the presupposition that even supposed akratic motivation is subject to assessment. For example, Alfred Mele's[24] recent work on "motivational balance" and "resistance strategies", in which the agent attempts to resist akratic desires, presupposes an assessment of various motivations. The "resistance strategies" seem to simply serve to influence this assessment in a particular direction - away from "akratic desire" toward "better judgement". This phenomenon is also clear in Herbert Fingarette's <u>Heavy Drinking</u>[25], in which he describes organizations such as Alcoholics Anonymous as overcoming weakness of will through strengthening the agent's assessment of alternative motivation.

It would seem that the presence of non-cognitive desires are simply "facts", which may or may not influence the agent in question when he determines what action to take. On this model, it is the agent's assessment which acts as "helmsman". While desires and other facts may potentially lead to action, these external considerations only motivate if attached to an appropriate assessment by the agent. In this way, external considerations merely influence the agent's determination of action; the agent's own evaluative assessment remains "helmsman".

There are, however, cases wherein these external influences are so extreme that they may threaten autonomy; when "no sensible man" could choose otherwise. In such cases, the agent's behavior reflects more the circumstances at hand than the agent's practical wisdom, and so the agent cannot be said to act as "helmsman" of his own conduct. When external influences do not act as helmsman in this way, they do not threaten the agent's autonomy.

In this regard, the only type of akrasia we might take seriously is something akin to that offered by Donald Davidson.[26] Davidson attempts to salvage the concept of weakness of will from the type of conflation I have been alluding to. Davidson characterizes weakness of will in terms of irrationality. Weakness of will is when an agent has a reason for doing X, but no reason for doing X *rather than* Y (when Y is a better alternative).

Let me give an example of the sort of case I believe Davidson has in mind. I want ice cream, and there are two ice cream stores equally convenient to me. One is expensive, and gives small portions. The other is cheap and gives large portions. Both are equally good, and there is no other incentive to go to the store which serves smaller portions. Yet, I go to the store which serves smaller portions.

Davidson tells us that in these cases the agent's behavior is irrational. The agent has a reason for going to the ice cream store (she wants ice cream), but has no reason for going to *this* ice cream store, rather than the store which is cheaper and serves larger portions. Davidson tells us that any attempt to read reason into such behavior is bound to be frustrated.

Here, we can see a possible threat to the type of "sanity" and "reasonableness" we required of the "sensible" agent in the previous chapter. For example, Davidson's account would seem to capture the case of the person who places herself in a permanently vegetative state for no apparent reason other than a passing urge, when there are very important reasons not to (reasons which reflect fundamental human values and an appreciation of the type of creatures which human beings are).

However, even on a Davidsonian account, we must be careful not to require *too strong* of a notion of rationality. That is, we must not place the boundaries set by "sanity" and "reasonableness" too narrowly. While we may disagree with many assessments made by an agent which we feel are worse than they might have been (they are not reflective of "better judgement"), we usually understand the *structure* of this assessment, and understand human beings as the type of creatures who might make these assessments. We often act on the basis of desires, even to the detriment of "better judgement": Hill's examples are familiar situations. But we understand these only when the values threatened are not in some sense *fundamental*. We do not understand the action of the woman who places herself in a permanently vegetative state on the basis of a passing urge as readily as we do the behavior of Amy in Hill's examples above. We do not readily relate to people who act in this way, because we find such assessments to be contrary to those which human beings might *understandably* make.

This is because certain boundaries are placed upon the type of assessments we can understand, in the manner described in the previous chapter. These boundaries separate "bad decisions" from decisions which lack an appreciation of the world and of human nature. For example, the man who satisfies the desire to eat in order to eliminate immediate hunger (to the detriment of his physique) is **not** in the same position as the woman who would place herself in a permanently vegetative state to satisfy a passing urge. The latter case lacks an appreciation of the world and human nature. As we discussed in the previous chapter, it lacks an appreciation of certain *fundamental* human values. Most concerns, like the concern for my physique, are not fundamental in this way.

In addition, we may not require that "rational" agents *optimize* in all situations. We simply are not the type of creatures who consistently optimize. For example, people adopt strategies for determining action (as we shall discuss in the next chapter), rules of thumb, and "satisfice" in many situations. Sometimes these strategies are adopted in order to "optimize" given the costs of *actually* optimizing in every situation. But other times these strategies are adopted simply because we find them convenient, or preferable, even when we believe their adoption is not "optimal".

Surely Davidson is right to maintain that we usually conceive of ourselves as rational creatures, and that rational behavior must be of the type he broadly describes. But surely we do not believe that all of our actions are *optimally* rational. While it is true that most people would prefer their will to be rational in some "optimal" sense, and that we do, in fact, often look down on those who display an "irrational" will of this type, we surely do not find people who do not optimize to be acting contrary to human nature, or to be "insane". Are their wills weak? I would think that they are not; it seems that this problem is tied to freedom of the will, rather than weakness of will.

To require optimality seems similar to the classical account of akrasia in an important respect. Both seem to want to characterize the "will" in certain terms, then define weakness of will in terms of this characterization. Just as the classical conception of Akrasia characterized the will in terms of "better judgement" *rather than* desire, requiring optimality characterizes the will in terms of what is optimal. When the will is not reflective of this characterization we have weakness of will. But it seems that what we really have is a case where we wish our will reflected this characteristic and it does not - a case of a lack of freedom of will.

In most cases, we find the behavior of individuals quite understandable, even when we realize the agent wishes she made different assessments. These cases of weakness of will are not threats to autonomy, as they demonstrate no lack of control *of an agent's evaluative assessments over her behavior*. At most, they demonstrate a problem of freedom of will.

Summary of "Part One: Autonomy"

The view of autonomy I have developed is based upon the metaphor of the "helmsman". This conception of autonomy is designed to avoid the many difficulties which are posed by the conception of "autonomy as autarkeia" when the latter conception is used for purposes in applied ethics. These problems include the vagueness of that concept in applied use, the austere existence required by such a rigorous notion, and the fundamental incompatibility of that notion with the various forms of authority and other external influences which serve important practical roles in the way we conduct our everyday lives.

Rather than requiring "detachment" from external influences as the conception of autonomy as autarkeia does, the concept of autonomy developed under the metaphor of the helmsman incorporates these influences into the autonomous determination of action. It is the active assessment of these influences, and the subsequent "steering" of behavior in the context of these influences, which constitutes autonomy. As "helmsman", the agent steers behavior in the midst of the practical concerns and considerations provided by these influences. Thus, the agent may steer her behavior in the light of the wishes and concerns of loved ones, the practical need for some forms of authority (such as physicians, or law, for example), and the practical consideration of the consequences of action.

Not all behavior, however, can be considered autonomous. Some behavior is compelled or coerced, and some forms of authority do in fact threaten autonomy (we shall take this up in detail in "Part Two: Authority"). The metaphor of the helmsman provides a way to distinguish such non-autonomous action from autonomous action. The distinction rests upon the question, "who (or what) acts as helmsman?". If the circumstances at hand or the commands of another person steer behavior, it cannot be considered autonomous. If the agent in question steers behavior, it is autonomous.

This requires that the agent retain control over her actions in the face of external influences. Thus, a "Humean" model of motivation, in which the agent's assessment is passive ("slave to passion") is incompatible with the helmsman metaphor. But this seems not to be a problem, as desires and other external influences do seem subject to an agent's assessment. This can be seen not only through the need to account for the idea of "strength of desire", but also is evidenced by the fact that even so-called "weakness of will" can be overcome through appropriate assessments on the part of the agent.

[1] Kant, Grounding for the Metaphysics of Morals, p.27.
[2] Kant, Grounding for the Metaphysics of Morals, p.50.
[3] Kant, Grounding for the Metaphysics of Morals, p.8.
[4] See Pettit, Philip "Humeans, Anti-Humeans, and Motivation", Mind (1987);

Smith, Michael "The Humean Theory of Motivation" Mind (1987), and "On Humeans, Anti-Humeans, and Motivation: A Reply to Pettit" Mind (1988).

[5] See Wilkerson, T.E. "Desire, Belief and Rational Action", Ratio XXVIII (Dec.1986).

[6] See my discussion of Dworkin's position in chapter one.

[7] See Charles Taylor, "Responsibility for Self", in A.E. Rorty, ed., The Identities of Persons (Berkeley: University of California Press, 1976), pp.281-299.

[8] Such as Joseph Butler; See Frey, R.G. "Butler on Self-Love and Benevolence", Unpublished paper.

[9] Wolf, Susan "Sanity and the Metaphysics of Responsibility", in Schoeman, Ferdinand (ed.), Responsibility, Character and the Emotions, (New York: Cambridge University Press, 1987), p.52.

[10] Davidson, Essays on Actions and Events, Oxford University Press (1980) p.xii.

[11] I have benefitted greatly in understanding this danger from discussions with Antony Flew, who warns that suggesting that the distinction between motivation and causation is a distinction between different sorts of causing, rather than different senses of the word "cause", facilitates the confusion that there is a cause/effect relationship between reasons for action and action which is the same as that between physical events. See, for example, Flew, Antony and Vesey, Godfrey Agency and Necessity (Oxford: Basil Blackwell, 1987), p.55.

[12] Davidson, "Actions, Reasons, and Causes", and "How is Weakness of the Will Possible?", both in Essays on Actions and Events (New York: Oxford University Press, 1980).

[13] Aristotle, Nicomachean Ethics, bk.VII.

[14] Aquinas, Summa Theologica Part II.

[15] See Davidson, Donald "How is Weakness of the Will Possible?" in Essays on Actions and Events, (New York: Oxford University Press, 1980) for a more detailed account of this characterization of Akrasia in terms of a struggle between reason and desire.

[16] I take this quote from Davidson's "How is Weakness of the Will Possible?". Davidson quotes the passage from Austin's "A Plea for Excuses", p.146.

[17] Watson, "Free Agency", p.85.

[18] Hill, Thomas "Weakness of Will and Character", in Autonomy and Self Respect (New York: Cambridge University Press, 1991) pp.118-137.

[19] Hill, "Weakness of Will and Character", p.120.

[20] Hill, "Weakness of Will and Character", p.120.

[21] Hill, "Weakness of Will and Character", pp.120-121.

[22] Hill, "Weakness of Will and Character", p.121.

[23] Hill, "Weakness of Will and Character", p.121.

[24] Mele, Alfred Irrationality (New York: Oxford University Press, 1987).

[25] Fingarette, Herbert Heavy Drinking (Berkeley: University of California Press, 1988).

[26] Davidson, Donald "How is Weakness of the Will Possible?", in Essays on Actions and Events (New York: Oxford University Press, 1980).

PART TWO:
AUTHORITY

INTRODUCTION TO PART TWO

INTRODUCTION TO PART TWO

Throughout this work we have been concerned with an understanding of the concept of autonomy in the context of the various external considerations which influence our behavior. Such an understanding of autonomy is vital if the concept is to serve in the prominent role it now assumes in applied ethics. In this context, a viable concept of autonomy cannot require the rigorous detachment which characterizes the concept of "autonomy as *autarkeia*" (the conception which underpins the most influential modern works on autonomy). In its place, I have offered a conception of autonomy as "self-rule", which models autonomous behavior in terms of "the metaphor of the helmsman". This conception of autonomy offers an understanding of the concept which can distinguish autonomous from non-autonomous behavior in a way more consistent with our ordinary understanding of the concept and the ways in which we employ this concept to practical moral issues.

Adopting a conception of autonomy modeled upon the metaphor of the helmsman allows an understanding of autonomous behavior compatible with the influence of external considerations. This compatibility is achieved in a way which is simultaneously plausible in the context of ordinary usage of the concept, and devoid of the paradoxical positions thrust upon a rigorous notion of self-sufficiency. This is true because of the types of behavior we feel autonomous individuals engage in, the types of considerations upon which we feel autonomous individuals might act, and the necessity of some forms of authority for practical autonomy.

People act to satisfy desires, and to achieve (or avoid) certain consequences. To require detachment from these considerations is unrealistic. People act out of personal interests, or to please loved ones. To require detachment from these would make life austere. People appeal to moral schemata to make decisions. To require detachment from these might render life meaningless. People appeal to authority in various facets of life. To require detachment from this would require a person to become knowledgeable in too many areas, an expert in none. People can achieve autonomy in the world only in the context of an authoritative body of norms; this provides the stability which allows persons to direct their behavior in a viable manner.

All of the above characteristics fail the test of self-sufficiency. In this work, I have shown that a conception of autonomy modeled upon the helmsman metaphor can allow for these characteristics of actual people without conceptual threat to their autonomy. In this, the conception of autonomy modeled upon the helmsman metaphor can viably serve in a useful role in our understanding of, and struggles with, practical moral issues.

The helmsman metaphor adopts a much different attitude toward the affect which desires and the consequences of one's action have upon a person's determination of action. By positing autonomy as steering behavior within the context of these considerations, their influence does not pose a conceptual threat to self-rule. In fact, autonomy consists in the agent's steering by her understanding of these influences: toward certain consequences and the satisfaction of certain desires, and away from others.

This model presupposes a perspective in which desires and external considerations are not seen to "cause" behavior as physical events "cause" their effects. Rather, the agent assesses external considerations and steers action accordingly. I take this perspective as more plausible than a perspective such as that of the "Humean" (the perspective which leads Kant to formulate autonomy in terms of self-sufficiency). This plausibility is demonstrated through an examination of weakness of will, which is taken as an instance wherein the agent is said to be unable to steer her own behavior. I show that most accounts of weakness of will do not indicate that an agent has relinquished control over the direction of her behavior, but rather suffers from a lack of control in terms of freedom of will. Autonomy is concerned with freedom of action. I have shown this distinction to be vital if we are to develop a viable, *practical* understanding of responsibility for use in structuring society.

Besides providing a plausible conception of autonomous practical reasoning, which is the primary focus of "Part One: Autonomy", the model of autonomy in terms of helmsmanship can help us to understand when certain obligations and requirements are compatible with autonomy. This compatibility is the focus of "Part Two: Authority". Obligations provide agents with certain types of reasons for action: namely, "second-order" reasons for action.

The model of obligations as second-order reasons which operates throughout part two of this work provides a way to understand obligations as compatible with autonomy, **if** the obligation allows the subject to steer her own behavior. In this way, our commitments to moral systems (such as religions), our appeals to various forms of authority (such as the authority of a physician), and our need for a system of authoritative norms (such as traffic law) are not set as a paradox in light of our conception of autonomy (as they are under a conception of "autonomy as *autarkeia*"). The resolution of the apparently paradoxical nature of these appeals, however, is tied to our understanding of autonomy modeled upon the helmsman metaphor. It is this model of autonomy which allows external considerations to influence an agent's determination of action without threat to her autonomy. The model of obligations as second-order reasons does not achieve self-sufficiency, but does allow us to view obligations as influencing *the agent's* determination of action, rather than *dictating* action.

There are two fundamentally different ways in which second-order reasons may function within an agent's practical reasoning. One way is consistent with the agent remaining "helmsman" of the direction of her behavior, and the other way replaces the agent as helmsman. Thus, if moral obligations provide requirements which function as the type of second-order reason which leaves the agent's helmsmanship intact, we can understand these obligations as compatible with autonomy. I then examine in detail how moral obligations may (and may not) be understood to function as the type of second-order reason which leaves the agent's helmsmanship intact. Those obligations which *are* consistent with the agent's helmsmanship are those which allow the agent to retain the prerogative to override the obligation on the basis of its justification.

The requirements of authority, however, pose a special problem to autonomy. The directive of an authority is understood to *replace* the agent's assessment of reasons for action, and thus threatens to replace the agent as helmsman in determining action. On close examination, however, the directives of authority can be understood in a way which does not threaten the agent's helmsmanship. The reasons which an authority's directive is meant to replace are **not** the reasons which justify the appeal to authority. Thus, if we understand authority as not precluding the agent's assessment of reasons to appeal to authority, the agent's helmsmanship is not threatened. This understanding of authority is based upon the understanding of obligation developed in the chapter preceding the examination of authority. It requires that the agent retain the prerogative to override the obligation which the authority's directive imposes, on the basis of the reasons which justify the agent's appeal to authority. If this prerogative is retained, the obligation to obey authority functions as the type of second-order reason which leaves the agent's helmsmanship intact.

Finally, the obligations imposed by an authoritative body of norms seem especially problematic. This is so because the purpose of such norms seems undermined if agents retain the prerogative to override the obligation to conform. For example, the usefulness of an authoritative body of traffic law is tied to our ability to *count* upon compliance by others. If compliance by others is subject to the unique circumstances (or whatever might override the obligation to obey) of these other agents, we lose the ability to *count* upon their compliance. Thus, a system of norms which is compatible with autonomy seems to lose much of its usefulness.

However, I demonstrate that a proper understanding of the obligation to obey authoritative societal norms, specifically the legal system, must be developed on a two-level model. The adoption of this two-level model allows the legal system to achieve the reliability required if this system of norms is to be effective, while simultaneously functioning as the type of second-order reason which does not threaten the agent's helmsmanship over her own behavior.

The understanding of autonomy modeled upon the metaphor of the helmsman, then, provides a plausible, *viable* conception of autonomy. It provides a conception of autonomy which allows us to view the normal behavior of actual people, behavior based upon concerns to satisfy certain desires, achieve certain consequences, or concerns about the welfare of ourselves or our loved ones, as autonomous behavior. In this, we may unproblematically understand these behaviors in the context of the ways we organize and structure society. In addition, it provides us with a model in which acting on certain obligations, and within the context of certain societal structures and appeals to authority, are consistent with autonomy. In this, we may develop an understanding of responsibility for behavior within these constraints, and an understanding of autonomous action which is not set as a paradox against the practical necessity for appeals to authority in the actual world.

CHAPTER FIVE
Autonomy and Normative Obligation

Thus far, I have set out to examine two opposing conceptions of autonomy. In doing so, I argued that a conception of autonomy as self-rule based upon the metaphor of the helmsman does not fall prey to the "dictates" of external influences in the manner feared by the view of autonomy as autarkeia. In this chapter, I shall turn my attention toward a specific type of external consideration, that of normative obligation.

This form of external consideration is very subtle, yet in many ways very pervasive. Obligation is a subtle form of external consideration in that it is exercised within the agent's own evaluative faculty. The agent must apply the normative requirements to his own evaluative assessments, and in this way appears to subvert his own evaluational judgement to that of the evaluational schema of the normative system in question. The application of normative principles to practical judgements, then, seems to pose a dilemma: either the agent subverts his own evaluational judgement to the (external) normative system, or he subverts normative requirements to his own evaluational judgement.

In his book Freedom and Reason,[1] R.M. Hare sets out to resolve what he sees as a paradox between freedom and reason in considering a moral problem. Hare sets up the paradox in the following manner:

> I wish to draw attention to two features which any such moral problem will have, the combination of which seems to confront us, as philosophers, with a paradox, or even an antinomy. The first is that a man who is faced with such a problem knows that it is his own problem, and that nobody can answer it for him.[2]

This embodies what Hare takes to be the aspect of freedom which allows for the determination of what action to take to be our own, and not "determined". But Hare goes on to pit this notion of autonomous determination of action against the requirements of reason in morality:

> Against this conviction, which every adult has, that he is free to form his own opinions about moral questions, we have to set another characteristic of these questions which

> seems to contradict it. This is, that the answering of moral questions is, or ought to be, a rational activity. Although most of us think that we are free to form our own opinions about moral questions, we do not feel that it does not matter what we think about them - that the answering of moral questions is a quite arbitrary business... We feel, rather, that it matters very much what answer we give, and that the finding of an answer is a task that should engage our rational powers to the limit of their capacity.[3]

In setting up this apparent paradox, Hare identifies a fundamental problem for autonomy in regard to moral principles. In brief, can adherence to a moral system be consistent with personal autonomy, or does autonomous judgement require the moral standard itself be determined by the agent? For if one's practical evaluations are directed by some moral system, in what sense can an agent be said to determine his own action?

Hare's presentation of this apparent paradox is raised in the context of meta-ethics, and our understanding of the nature of moral judgements. But the problem is also present at the level of substantive moral theory. For example, this problem is present in "Divine Command Theories" of moral obligation, which have attempted to resolve the problem in various ways. The most prevalent attempts maintain that the directives of God are not inconsistent with moral autonomy, because they represent the law an autonomous person would give to himself. For example, take the following position:

> A reliance on something other than conscience is seen to threaten conscience's primacy. But if the independent basis of action is defined in such a way that it cannot conceivably violate conscience, then this problem and the threat vanish. In religious terms, this means that a God who is thought of, regarded, and defined as essentially moral can be an entirely acceptable source of moral direction because his commands must always correspond to what conscience requires.[4]

However, this approach to resolving the tension between autonomy and moral requirements will face the same difficulties which face Gerald Dworkin's account of autonomy (as discussed in chapter one). That is, this position has the relationship between autonomy and identification reversed. We identify with something *because* we choose it autonomously. Mere coincidence of what we *would have* chosen and what is required does not establish autonomy.[5]

The problem which faces any moral system in this context, is a problem which parallels that faced by the rigorous notion of "autonomy as autarkeia" when it encounters external influences. These problems stem from an emphasis on how one formulates one's principle of action. Recall that Kant's principle of autonomy required that one test one's action against a principle which was formulated by the agent himself, independently of external considerations. Upon this view, to determine action by some normative obligation not itself formulated by the agent in an autarkic manner would be to subvert the agent's autonomy. A principle of action which makes reference to the contingent commands of a Divine authority is not self-sufficient in this way. Likewise, Hare's apparent paradox also draws upon this concern with formulating one's principle of action. Hare's resolution of the apparent paradox rests upon his belief that moral judgements must meet certain formal requirements in order to qualify as moral. It is through the formal requirements that the "objective" character is added to the agent's moral judgement. But it is also here that the question must be raised concerning the direction of moral determinations: Can the standard of moral judgement itself be objective and yet consistent with the agent's autonomy?

The key to addressing this question is to understand the problem in terms of practical reason, rather than in terms of the formulation of one's principle of action. This shift away from a concern with the formulation of one's principle of action parallels the shift away from "autonomy as autarkeia" toward "autonomy as self-rule". If we again shift our concern away from autarkeia to self-rule, allowing that external considerations may influence the determination of action if attached to an appropriate assessment by the agent, we may understand normative obligations as a type of external consideration which does not pose the apparent paradox considered above.

Although we have rejected the "Humean" picture of desire-based motivation, the model I have proposed retains Hume's contention that *facts* as such are motivationally inert. In order to result in motivation, the discernment of some fact must be subject to the agent's evaluative assessments. Normative standards are no different than any other fact. To guide conduct, they must be assessed as relevant by the agent in question.

However, requiring that normative obligations (as external considerations) be attached to an agent's assessment in this way seems, at first glance, to miss the point of normative obligations: they are meant to *structure* an agent's assessments. To view these obligations as themselves simply a factor in the agent's assessments, is to fail to appreciate how normative obligations function. Let us look at this more closely.

Suppose that Smith must decide whether or not to contribute his time to the local youth organization. In making his decision, Smith decides that he attaches little value to helping the youth of the community, and ultimately decides against donating his time. This is an example of an agent's evaluative assessment. It is upon this evaluation that Smith determines his course of action.

Now suppose that the local minister declares Smith's decision to be "reprehensible". He *should have*, asserts the minister, attached greater value to helping the community's youth. This is an example of what I call normative assessment. This assessment holds that certain considerations should carry a certain weight.

It is important to notice in these two types of assessment wherein the emphasis lies. While an agent's evaluative assessment is concerned with the actual determination of action, normative assessment is concerned with what considerations should carry what weight: it is meant to *structure* an agent's evaluative assessments. For example, the minister in the above case believes that the principle of altruism should play a greater role in Smith's practical reasoning.

I will below offer a model for understanding normative obligations in terms of second-order reasons. These reasons, which concern the structure of assessment of first-order reasons, can provide a model for understanding the relationship between normative requirements and an agent's evaluative assessments which is able both to connect the normative requirement to the agent's evaluative assessments in a way which allows us to view it as an external consideration, and to do this while simultaneously capturing the proper function of normative requirements as *structuring* an agent's evaluative assessments.

On this model, the function of normative requirements is captured by a sophisticated understanding of the agent's own practical reasoning, in which she adopts certain strategies for structuring her (first-order) assessments which, I shall argue, might reflect her own evaluative assessments. The issue of whether the normative requirement threatens her autonomy, then, centers around the way that requirement operates within this sophisticated understanding of her practical reasoning. In this, the model shifts the focus of the relationship between an agent's evaluations and normative requirements away from how the normative standards are themselves formulated, and to how these standards operate within an agent's practical reasoning.

In shifting the emphasis away from the formulation of one's principle of action to actual practical evaluation, the apparent paradox of autonomy and objectivity disappears. As an external influence on the agent, the application of objective moral standards might be seen as compatible with autonomy. An agent may decide to evaluate various alternatives in a particular way because of a strong religious belief, for example, and structure the determination of her action accordingly. As we shall see, this action might well be autonomous.

Where the authority of moral principles *might* pose a problem to autonomy, however, is if the moral principle goes beyond providing a standard for the agent to apply to his practical evaluation, and instead itself acts as helmsman in the determination of action. Just as other external considerations may eliminate the agent from acting as "Helmsman", so too might normative obligation. Let us now develop this model.

Practical Reason and Obligation

Thus far, I have simply attempted to show that the traditional approach to the question concerning the compatibility of autonomy with normative obligations is misguided. Autonomous judgement does *not* require the standards of value be grounded subjectively. To clearly understand the threat that normative obligations may pose to autonomy, we must examine the way in which these obligations function in the context of an agent's practical reasoning, and determine whether they eliminate the agent's own evaluational judgement from acting as helmsman in the determination of action.

Normative standards are prescriptive in nature. By this, I mean that normative standards attempt to identify appropriate considerations upon which to act. The danger which normative standards pose to autonomy must be recognized through the question of who acts as helmsman or, in this case, who makes the assessment of various reasons for action? If the normative standard is to make an assessment, it must not replace the agent's assessment of what action to take and therefore replace the agent as helmsman.

I shall argue that normative standards do not need to eliminate an agent's evaluative assessment from the determination of action. Normative standards are but a sophisticated type of reason for action, and thus are simply facts like any other reason for action. The difference they have from other reasons for action is that they operate at a different level - as second order reasons - but they are reasons for action nonetheless. As second-order reasons, normative standards are reasons to attach certain weight to first-order reasons for action. Still, it is the agent who assesses these second-order reasons, and so long as they do not threaten this role as helmsman (but merely influence her as another type of external consideration), they are perfectly consistent with autonomy. We shall examine below how second-order reasons might (and might not) reflect the agent's active evaluative assessment.

Although the notion of second-order reasons was recognized as a significant contribution to philosophical work in the area of practical reason and action, it has never received its proper due as a tool for understanding how obligations affect moral reasoning. Joseph Raz[6] was one of the first to explore how the notion of second order reasons can help us to understand the nature of obligations and how they effect practical reason. However, there remains confusion as to exactly how we are to understand what a second-order reason is, and how it relates to other reasons we have to perform various actions.

The various examples used by Raz to illustrate second-order reasoning emphasize different aspects of the relationship of second-order reasons to other reasons for action we may have; that diversity clouds the role second-order reasons play within practical reason. At times, it seems that second-order reasons are phenomena of indirect strategies to achieve an end which an individual may not achieve through direct strategy in determining action. Yet other times it seems that second-order reasons impose obligations independent of other reasons and strategies for achieving a given end.

In the following sections, I will examine the concept of second-order reasons, and attempt to clarify this notion by maintaining that the apparent ambiguity in the examples of second-order reasons given by Raz is due to the different ways this type of reason might relate to other reasons for action. This distinction, which Raz himself seems to have overlooked, can help to identify the types of obligations which are and are not compatible with autonomy.

The Concept of Second-Order Reasons

Raz explains second-order reasons as reasons to act on particular reasons for action or to refrain from acting on particular reasons for action.[7] In this way, second-order reasons can be distinguished from first-order reasons in that, whereas a first-order reason affects our determination of action through the weight of that reason, second-order reasons affect our determination of action through the affect the (second-order) reason has on other (primarily first-order) reasons.

Raz gives several examples to illustrate the concept of second-order reasons. The first of these is the case of Ann, who attempts to determine whether or not to take a proposed investment opportunity:

> Imagine the case of Ann who is looking for a good way to invest her money. Late one evening a friend tells her of a possible investment. The snag is that she has to decide that same evening for the offer to make the deal will

be withdrawn at midnight. The proposed investment is a very complicated one, that much is clear to Ann. She is aware that it may be a very good investment, but there may be facts which may mean that it will not be a good bargain for her after all, and she is not certain whether it is better or worse than another proposition which was put to her a few days before and which she is still considering. All she requires is a couple of hours of thorough examination of the two propositions. All the relevant information is available in the mass of documents on her table. But Ann has had a long and strenuous day with more than the average amount of emotional upsets. She tells her friend that she cannot take a rational decision on the merits of the case since even were she to try and work out the consequences of accepting the offer she would not succeed; she is too tired and upset to trust her own judgement. He replies that she cannot avoid taking a decision. Refusing to consider the offer is tantamount to rejecting it. She admits that she rejects the offer but says that she is not doing it because she thinks the reasons against it override those in its favor but because she cannot trust her own judgement at this moment.[8]

In the above example, the basis of Ann's decision to reject the proposed investment offer is not the weights of the various reasons for and against making the investment. Rather, Ann has a reason (she is tired and cannot trust her own judgment) which affects the reasons for and against making the investment. That Ann is tired and cannot trust her own judgement is a *second-order* reason to *not act on certain other reasons* for accepting or rejecting the proposed investment.

In this example, the second-order reason functions as an indirect strategy. Ann obviously wishes to get the highest return on her investment. The determination of which investment opportunity will benefit her most (the investment proposed by her friend or the other proposition which was put to her a few days before) would normally be calculated by evaluating each alternative in regard to the end to be achieved.

However, because Ann is tired and does not trust her own judgement, she maintains that she will likely fail to correctly determine which investment would result in the best consequences. Therefore, she feels that she will benefit most by not attempting to calculate which investment will benefit her most at this time, *precisely because she does not trust her own judgement*. This reason affects the weight of the reasons for taking or not taking the proposed investment by making them irrelevant to her determination of action.

A Second Concept of Second-order Reasons

Later in the same chapter of <u>Practical Reason and Norms</u>, Raz offers another example of a second-order reason which seems to function in a slightly different way:

> ...consider the case of Colin who promised his wife that in all decisions affecting the education of his son he will act only for his son's interests and disregard all other reasons. Suppose Colin has now to decide whether or not to send his son to a public school. Among the relevant reasons are the fact that if he does he will be unable to resign his job in order to write the book he so much wants to write, and the fact that given his prominent position in his community his decision will affect the decisions of quite a few other parents, including some who could ill afford the expense. However, he believes that because of his promise he should disregard such considerations altogether (unless, that is, they have indirect consequences affecting his son's welfare). Again, some will think that his promise is not binding, but that is beside the point. Our aim is simply to understand the reasoning of those who believe in such reasons, and it must be admitted that they are numerous.[9]

Again in this example, the agent's reason for action (Colin's promise) does not determine the agent's action directly, but rather serves as a reason for the agent to act for a particular reason for action (for the reason 'that it is in his son's interests') and exclude other reasons for action which the agent may have from his determination of action. Colin's promise influences his determination of action through its affect on other (first-order) reasons for action (it is a reason to act for a particular first order reason and exclude others), and thus is a second-order reason.

Although there are obviously many similarities between the case of Ann and the case of Colin,[10] there are also important differences. Foremost among these is the fact that in the case of Colin, the second-order reason in question does not appear to function as an indirect strategy, but rather seems to *change the normative situation* by establishing new criteria by which to determine action.

While in the case of Ann the second-order reason did not change the end to be achieved (but only changed the strategy to achieve this end), the case involving Colin is quite different. Here it appears that by placing an obligation upon Colin to decide on the basis of his son's welfare, the second-order reason (Colin's promise to act only for his son's interests and to disregard other reasons) does not change the strategy by which to achieve the end Colin would normally pursue,[11] but instead changes the very end which Colin is to pursue.

As these two examples illustrate, there seem to be two ways in which second-order reasons might affect the weight of first-order reasons. Second-order reasons as indirect strategies affect first-order reasons by affecting the weights to be assigned to each reason in relation to the end to be aimed at. Because the new strategy does not weigh the pros and cons for or against each investment proposition, the first-order reasons no longer carry any weight (they are no longer relevant to the determination of action); not because the end has changed, but because the strategy to achieve the end has changed (I no longer attempt to determine the balance of reasons).

However, the above description is different than the way in which Colin's promise affects the weight of first-order reasons. Colin's promise, as I have discussed, changes *the end to be aimed at*. Therefore, first-order reasons which carry weight in relation to the end which would otherwise be aimed at (were the second-order reason not present) do not carry the same weight; for the end to be aimed at has changed, and so too, therefore, have the strength of (first-order) reasons for action in relation to this new end. For example, if the end I aim at is to become very heavy, the first-order reasons to eat may be very weighty indeed. However, if the end I aim at changes to becoming physically fit, the first-order reasons I have to eat will accordingly lose considerable weight relative to this new end.

The Importance of the Distinction

The above cases illustrate two fundamentally different ways in which second-order reasons can function within an agent's practical reasoning. As I shall discuss below, indirect strategies do not eliminate an agent's practical evaluation from the determination of action in the manner that Colin's promise does. Although Colin's promise may be taken as a second-order reason because of Colin's evaluation that it should be taken as such, it nevertheless then *replaces* Colin's evaluational judgement in the practical evaluation of alternatives; the second order reason identifies what facts are relevant to Colin's determination of action. In this, Colin's promise shares with the Kantian categorical imperative an emphasis on Colin's formulation of the principle of action (Colin's judgement established the promise as a second-order reason), and lack of concern for whether this principle of action then eliminates Colin's evaluational judgement from the practical determination of action.

The difference in the ways second order reasons might function in the context of an agent's practical reason is especially apparent when attempting to understand the way normative principles operate in the context of practical reasoning. Normative principles which operate as indirect strategies are affected by different sorts of considerations than are normative principles which operate as imperatives (such as Colin's promise). A second-order reason which functions as an indirect strategy will be affected by considerations which indicate that the indirect strategy the second-order reason represents is not, in fact, the appropriate strategy for achieving the end desired. Thus, considerations such as the fact that no investment opportunities will be available if Ann does not decide right away may indicate that a strategy of 'not weighing the pros and cons for taking an investment at the present time' is not the strategy which will likely give her the best results, even though Ann remains tired (either investment may be considered better than no investment). Second-order reasons which function as indirect strategies may be undermined through reference to the end that the agent's own evaluational judgement establishes. Thus, such indirect strategies allow the agent's own practical evaluation to continue to determine action. Since the second order reason does not affect the actual end to be achieved, the second order reason does not inhibit the agent from changing his or her practical evaluation of various alternatives on the basis of this end. The agent still evaluates what facts are relevant to her determination of action.

Second-order reasons which function as imperatives, however, are not susceptible to such considerations. A second-order reason which functions as an imperative *establishes* the end to be achieved, and so considerations which are based upon the original end aimed at have no affect upon the second-order reason. In this way, then, imperatives eliminate the agent's practical evaluation from influencing the determination of action. Although the agent's practical evaluation may establish the second order reason, this kind of second order reason establishes an end which is then independent of the influence of the agent's practical faculty. The imperative identifies what to attach value to, rather than the agent.

Let us consider an example to illustrate the difference between these two types of second-order reasons. Suppose Colin's promise, to act on the basis of his son's interests in matters affecting his son, is adopted as an indirect strategy. Perhaps because Colin does not hold a position of importance in the community, and because other influences on his decisions are also insignificant, and because it takes a great deal of time to actually balance these considerations, Colin determines that in matters affecting his son, it would be best to simply adopt a strategy of acting on the basis of his son's interests. Since his son's interests hold great value for Colin, this strategy will most likely give the result Colin wishes (just as Ann's strategy was adopted because she believed her goal would most likely be achieved through it, given her tired condition).

Now suppose Colin's circumstances change, in that his position in the community becomes significant; so significant that his decision's affect on the community becomes, in the greater scheme of things, even more important to Colin than his son's interests. Colin will now likely determine that his strategy of always acting on the basis of his son's interests will not be likely to give him the appropriate result. That strategy, then, will likely be discarded.

However, if Colin's promise is adopted as an "imperative", he cannot discard the strategy on the basis of the change in his position in the community. His promise is to act on the basis of his son's interests, and to take that as his end. His own evaluation of what is more important, then, is no longer reflected by the strategy. This fact illustrates that the decisions taken under the direction of this strategy are not *decisions* which reflect Colin's ends (although the adoption of the strategy itself does). Rather, the decision taken under the direction of the strategy in question reflects the end established by *the strategy*. And this end might or might not coincide with Colin's. Evidence that it does not, unlike the affect of such evidence on indirect strategies, does not affect the strategy's application.

Thus, second order reasons which function as imperatives are analogous to placing oneself on "automatic pilot". While the second-order reason may be adopted on the basis of the agent's own evaluational judgement, the agent's judgement is then eliminated from the practical determination of action.

Normative Principles

This distinction I have drawn can most readily be seen by reference to principles adopted by rule-consequentialists and principles adopted by Kantians. Rule-consequentialist principles function as indirect strategies to achieve given consequences. Kantian principles (or categorical imperatives), whatever the reason for their presence, function as imperatives. Thus, the obligation imposed by a rule-consequentialist principle against lying is much different than a Kantian principle of the same nature. This difference is most clear when we ask what might justify lying (and thus undermine the principle against lying) in each case.

For the rule-consequentialist, the principle against lying is susceptible to consideration of consequences. The rule-consequentialist may place great weight upon following rules even to some disadvantage, but there will eventually come a point at which the negative consequences of following a rule will force the rule-consequentialist to concede that following the rule is not the thing to do. The agent's evaluational judgement continues to "trump" the rule.

A Kantian, on the other hand, will view a categorical imperative as a principle to be followed *whatever the consequences*. There is no point, for the Kantian, at which he must concede that following the rule will no longer achieve the end to be aimed at. This is because conformity to the rule, for the Kantian, **is** the end to be aimed at. In this, the agent's evaluational judgement is eliminated from the practical determination of action. The rule "trumps" the agent's evaluational judgement.

As autonomy is embodied in action which results from the agent's evaluational judgement, only obligations which function as a second-order reason which does not "trump" the agent's evaluational judgement is consistent with autonomy. Thus, the system of authoritative rules by which we govern society may recognize the normative force of various "objective" obligations and other normative requirements, so long as the nature of these obligations are taken as second-order reasons functioning within the agent's practical reasoning as an indirect strategy.

This will become even more clear in the next chapter, as we examine the obligation imposed by authoritative directives, and how the requirement of action by authority may (and may not) be consistent with the autonomy of the subject. Authority is exercised through an appeal for compliance which is based upon an obligation to do as directed by the authority. This obligation might be justified by prudential rationality (as in the case of a physician, for example); by moral beliefs (like the religious obligations we have examined in this chapter); or by virtually any consideration which might provide an agent with a reason to appeal to authority. If these reasons are weighty enough to oblige one to appeal to authority (according to the "Normal Justification Thesis" which we shall examine in the next chapter), the appeal for compliance is established. Let us now turn to this model of authority.

¹Hare, R.M., Freedom and Reason, (New York: Oxford University Press, 1963).
²Hare, Freedom and Reason, p.1.
³Hare, Freedom and Reason, p.2-3.
⁴Green, Ronald M. "Abraham, Isaac, and the Jewish Tradition: An Ethical Reappraisal", The Journal of Religious Ethics, vol.10, no.1 (Spring 1982, pp.1-21), p.17. See also Robert M. Adams's discussion of various attempts to resolve this problem in The Virtue of Faith (New York: Oxford University Press, 1987).
⁵See the discussion of autonomy and identification in chapter one.
⁶See Raz, Joseph Practical Reason and Norms (London: Hutchinson, 1975; reprinted by Princeton University Press, 1990).
⁷Raz, Joseph Practical Reason and Norms, p.39
⁸Raz, Practical Reason and Norms, p.37.
⁹Raz, Practical Reason and Norms, p.39.
¹⁰These similarities include the fact that in neither case is the subject acting on "the balance of reasons", and in each case, the second-order reason operates by affecting the weight of first-order reasons, making at least some irrelevant to the subject's determination of action.
¹¹We must assume in this instance that it is not, or at least need not, be his son's interests to the exclusion of all other reasons that would dictate action normally. Otherwise, it is difficult to understand just what a promise is. It seems that a promise only is relevant if the action required by the promise is somehow at odds with the action that would be done were the promise not present (even if this is only to say that the promise significantly reinforced the conviction with which the action is determined).

CHAPTER SIX
Authority and Obligation

Can an effective authority be compatible with the autonomy of those subject to authority? The above is an important question, for in many respects authority looks to be a necessary part of our everyday lives. The authority of traffic law, for example, seems necessary if we wish to co-ordinate the actions of individual drivers so that we may safely get from one place to another. Although in some sense it is true that the traffic law restricts my behavior (I may not drive on a certain side of the road), in another sense it seems my freedom is enhanced by the presence of this authority (the co-ordination of my action with that of others allows me to go places I would not otherwise be able to go). Some forms of authority, like the authority of traffic law, seem to both enhance and limit my autonomy. If autonomy and authority are fundamentally incompatible (as many writers believe they are[1]), we are faced with a serious paradox concerning individual freedom.

In this chapter, I will examine various attempts to reconcile autonomy and authority. I will first examine attempts to reconcile these concepts through the nature of the directives which an authority issues. Showing these to fail, I then examine the notion of authority developed by Joseph Raz, and particularly focus upon his notion of the Dependence Thesis, which places certain limitations upon what the directives of an authority should reflect. After examining several shortcomings in Raz's version of the Dependence Thesis, I then offer a modified Dependence Thesis which overcomes these shortcomings, and allows us to understand authority in such a way that, given certain limitations, the autonomy of the subject can be recognized without sacrificing the effective obligation authority imposes upon the subject to comply.

The Nature of Authority

The term 'authority' is often used in a variety of contexts. At times, 'authority' is used to indicate status (such as the 'authority' of a police officer). At other times 'authority' is used to denote expertise in a given field (Einstein, for example, was an 'authority' on physics). In still other contexts the term 'authority' is used to indicate an ability to require action. It is this latter use which we shall be concerned with here.

We are concerned with authority as it affects the autonomy of those subject to the authority. Thus, we shall not be concerned with 'authority' as the term is used to denote status, for this use of the term is primarily concerned with 'authorization', focusing on the normative questions surrounding *the actions of the authority* (was the action done by commission, or license, etc.?). We are concerned with the normative questions surrounding *the actions of the subject.*

Likewise, we shall not be concerned with 'authority' as the term is employed to denote expertise, except in the indirect way in which expertise may impose an obligation to do as directed by the person who has this expertise (for example, the expertise of a physician may impose an obligation upon a nurse to implement prescribed treatments). We shall not be concerned with the simple denotation of expertise.

We shall be concerned with 'authority' as the term is used to indicate the ability to require action. Such an ability raises questions concerning the autonomy of the subject, because the ability to require action does not seem to allow the subject to determine for himself what action to engage in.

Let us examine, then, 'authority' as it is used in this context. Authority, it seems, requires action by imposing an obligation on the subject to comply with the directives of the authority. Joseph Raz describes the authority's ability to require action as identical to her ability to impose this obligation:

> The obligation to obey authority is the obligation to obey
> if and when the authority commands. This is the same as
> a power or capacity in the authority to issue valid or binding directives.[2]

In being exercised through obligation, authority shares with obligation the characteristic of being exercised within the agent's own practical faculty. In this, authority is an appeal for compliance, rather than physical force or compulsory power:

> It seems the justified use of coercive power is one thing
> and authority is another. I do not exercise authority over

people afflicted with dangerous diseases if I knock them out and lock them up to protect the public, even though I am, in the assumed circumstances, justified in doing so. I have no more authority over them than I have over mad dogs. The exercise of coercive or any other form of power is no exercise of authority unless it includes an appeal for compliance by the person(s) subject to the authority. That is why the typical exercise of authority is through giving instructions of one kind or another. But appeal to compliance makes sense precisely because it is an invocation of the duty to obey.[3]

The obligation to obey an authority is an obligation to take the reason provided by the authority's directive as one's reason for action, and to perform the act directed by the authority. Thus, the subject in some sense *surrenders* his own determination of action to the authority. Let me illustrate this with the following passage from The Morality of Freedom:

> Consider the case of two people who refer a dispute to an arbitrator. He has authority to settle the dispute, for they agreed to abide by his decision. Two features stand out. First, the arbitrator's decision is for the disputants a reason for action. They ought to do as he says because he says so. But this reason is related to the other reasons which apply to the case. It is not...just another reason to be added to the others, a reason to stand alongside the others when one reckons which way is better supported by reason. The arbitrator's decision is meant to be based on the other reasons, to sum them up and to reflect their outcome... This leads directly to the second distinguishing feature of the example. The arbitrator's decision is also meant to replace the reasons on which it depends. In agreeing to obey his decision they agree to follow his judgement of the balance of reasons rather than their own.[4]

For now we are concerned with what Raz sees as the 'second distinguishing feature' of the above example. By agreeing to abide by the authority's directive (in this case, the arbitrator's decision), the parties in question agree to obey the directive of the authority *whatever it may be*. This is a phenomenon H.L.A. Hart has termed a 'content independent reason'.[5]

It is easy to see why many philosophers maintain that obedience to authoritative directives is simply incompatible with autonomy. Acting on what the authority judges ought to be done appears to circumvent one's own evaluational judgement, and thus autonomy. By circumventing the evaluational judgment of the subject it seems the subject is *prevented* from acting on her own determination of what ought to be done. The subject seems to be eliminated from the determination of her behavior.

Varieties of Authoritative Directives

Before we examine how autonomy might be reconciled with authority, it would pay to first examine a variety of forms authoritative directives might take. This will serve two purposes. First, it will demonstrate the common problem which characterizes the antagonism between autonomy and authority across the various forms of directives: can authority require action and remain compatible with autonomy?

Second, in examining how the various forms of authoritative directives fall prey to the same antagonism with autonomy, we shall examine (and reject) a variety of attempts to reconcile autonomy with authority through the nature of the directives issued by the authority. In this, we may better clarify the antagonism of autonomy and authority, and the issue(s) around which any reconciliation of these concepts must revolve. We shall begin with the most general form of authoritative directive: the simple requirement of action.

The Simple Requirement of Action

Requiring specific action is perhaps the simplest and most straightforward form of authoritative directive. This type of directive demands certain actions be performed by the subject, and thus seems to circumvent the subject's own practical faculty.

In an unpublished paper,[6] James Child of Bowling Green State University maintains that not only is autonomy *possible* in carrying out the commands of an authority, but that the implementation of the command *requires* some degree of (minimal) autonomy. Child begins by making a distinction between "immediate" and "ultimate" authority. He explains these concepts as follows:

> The general who commands the brigade has ultimate authority over the brigade. However, with the general's concurrence or within areas set out by him, the colonel, as deputy commander, might have immediate authority. He directly gives instructions to the brigade, for example. The prosecutor in a trial has immediate authority to direct questions to the witness but the judge has ultimate authority.[7]

Using this distinction, Child goes on to develop obedience to authority as a phenomenon requiring a type of immediate authority within the context of the ultimate authority of the person issuing the command:

> A Marine sergeant shouts in the ear of a recruit, "Come to attention". This is ultimate authority in its most unequivocal form. Still, it is the recruit who must snap his eyes forward, pull back his shoulders, suck in his stomach, place his feet parallel, one foot apart, etc....the sergeant will give the order "Attention!" and the recruit will exercise his immediate authority over those voluntary bodily movements which are constitutive of the action of coming to attention. In this very basic and very thin sense, authority presupposes autonomy.[8]

In this way, Child's conception of autonomy appears to be perfectly consistent with the original idea of autonomy as presented by Macken, and upon which I have developed a theory of autonomy as practical reason; autonomy is "immediate authority" within the larger framework of "ultimate authority". However, I think Child fails to recognize an important aspect of the examples of immediate authority which he gives. By immediate authority, I take it that Child wishes to develop the idea that even (some of) those under an obligation to others may have authority over their own actions to some extent. For example, the platoon leader "steers" the actions of the platoon, while the General "steers" the actions of the army as a whole. To the extent that the platoon leader may determine what to do (e.g. "take a hill"), the platoon leader has "immediate" authority.

However, the recruit in Child's example fails to possess the ability to steer his own behavior in any viable sense. Child himself admits that while it is true that the recruit could simply refuse to obey and suffer the consequences, this is a somewhat "artificial" option.[9] However, Child feels that in processing the information, interpreting this information, and *deciding how to implement the orders*, the recruit exercises a degree of (minimal) autonomy.

I disagree with Child's assessment. It seems that the recruit's steering is but an illusion, because he does not in any viable sense determine what to do. The recruit is more analogous to a slave than to the platoon leader. The importance of this is especially clear in the context of Aristotle's discussion of slavery; Aristotle viewed the artisan as a type of slave labor (Pol.1278a5-10) because he sees the artisan as a mechanic, and thus not something to which the concepts of virtue and merit can apply (Pol.1278a15-20).

This is important, for the recruit in Child's example no more determines his behavior than a "paint by numbers" artist determines what the painting she is working on shall look like. The recruit is given orders which require action. While it is true that he must process the orders, interpret the orders, and determine a means of compliance, in these activities the recruit's practical faculty is truly "slave" to the external considerations which make up the sergeant's command.

The sergeant's order must have an externally-determined interpretation if it is to direct at all; a directive that lacks meaningful content does not direct. For example, an order which commands one to "do as they judge they should do" would surely not threaten autonomy (the subject still determines what she should do); but it does this precisely because it fails to direct action. Likewise, the recruit's determination of how to comply with the order is dictated by what the order requires, and the circumstances he is in. While there may be more than one way in which the order may be carried out, the recruit's role in deciding this is no different than the artisan.

Sophisticated Directives

Some attempts to reconcile autonomy and authority have focused upon distinguishing *types* of authoritative directives (some types allowing the agent to retain the primary role in determining action). By making some types of directives limited in various ways, it is thought that the discretion of the agent is left intact.

However, I shall demonstrate that these "varieties" of authoritative directives are no more than sophisticated methods of requiring action. In this, such directives contain the same structural features of obligation and practical reason that characterize simple requirement of action, only in a more complicated form.

Conditional Directives

A conditional directive specifies action *in certain circumstances*. For example, an authority may direct me to "close the windows when it is raining". Under this directive, I am only obligated to engage in specific behavior (closing the windows) when certain conditions are present (when it is raining). When the conditions are not present, I am free to do as I please.

However, this type of directive does not serve to reconcile autonomy with authority. While it is true that my autonomy remains intact when the conditions established by the authority are not present, my autonomy remains intact precisely because I am not acting under an obligation imposed by the authority. The conditional directive establishes those conditions under which I am obligated to comply with the authority. When the conditions are not present, I am not obligated to comply. When the conditions are present, specific action is required.

Although the conditions established by the authority make the directive applicable only in certain circumstances, the fact that it specifies the conditions leaves little room (actually no room) for the subject to determine action when the conditions are present. However, it may be argued that the conditional nature of the directive requires the subject play a role in determining action by determining when the conditions are present. Take, for example, the following directive: "When Old Joe dies, foreclose on the ranch". In order to recognize an obligation to comply, I must first determine that Old Joe is dead.

However, while it is true that I must (under a conditional directive) make some practical judgement (for example, whether Old Joe is dead), it is not a *judgement* that I am able to influence in any way.[10] When all vital signs have stopped for a sufficient period of time, I am obligated to foreclose on the ranch.

In various facets of life, there are standards which are unique to that facet which are not standards in other facets of life. By this, I mean that meaning is often dependent on the context within which it is spoken. For instance, if I say that a sports figure is "over-the-hill, beyond his prime, no longer able to make a positive contribution", I refer to a specific facet of the sports figure's life. Within this facet, there are fairly well understood standards by which I evaluate this judgement of the ballplayer's value. If the utterance allows the subject to place whatever meaning he wishes on the "directive", it does not really impose obligation. To the extent that it does have meaning, it specifies action.

The Exclusion of Behavior Theory

Thus far, we have examined directives in which, when an obligation to comply is imposed, there is but one action which will constitute obedience. Thus, the directive "requires action". However, it is claimed that some types of directives are not closed-ended in this way. By remaining open-ended, these directives are claimed to leave the determination of action to the subject.

An 'open-ended' directive seems quite different from a directive which specifies action. Wherein a 'closed-ended' directive specifies what action would exclusively qualify as compliance, an 'open-ended' directive is said to specify what action would exclusively **not** qualify as compliance. In this way, 'open-ended' directives do not seem to require action, but rather simply set "bounds" on what actions an agent may engage in.

Let us look at an example of such an 'open-ended' directive: "Do not kill". At first glance, 'not killing' does not seem to be of the nature of 'foreclosing on the ranch'. There remains a wide range of options as to what to do, all of which are compatible with the authority's directive. In essence, the authority is said to direct the following: "Do what you judge you should do, but do not kill". The autonomy of the subject is thought to be left intact because the subject seems to remain "helmsman"; the authority's directive simply being another external consideration. Of a variety of possible alternative actions compatible with the directive, the subject determines which action to engage in.

The above describes what is known in jurisprudence as a 'general norm of permission'. The directive of the authority prohibits certain specific actions, and the subject is assumed to be permitted to engage in any activity not specifically prohibited in this manner. The subject simply excludes certain behavior from her range of possible actions, then determines her behavior from the range of options available after this exclusion. Compliance consists in accepting the obligation to limit behavior to those options available after the exclusion of certain behavior.

But it simply does not seem to be the case that I constantly exclude certain behavior from my range of options before I then determine what action to engage in. Rather, it seems more plausible that the directive only imposes an obligation when what I determine to do is in conflict with the authority's directive.

A much better way to articulate an intuitive sense of what it is I do when obeying an authority's open-ended directive is to refer once again to the concept of second order reasons I outlined earlier. There I described second order reasons as being "a reason to act for a reason or to refrain from acting for a reason". I described how compliance to a simple closed-ended directive constitutes a second order reason to act for a particular reason - that reason being "because the authority directed it". In the case of an open-ended directive, the authority's directive once again serves as a second order reason, but in this case it is a second order reason to refrain from acting for a particular reason. Specifically, an open-ended directive is a second order reason to refrain from acting on the reason that the balance of (first order) reasons is such that one should do those things prohibited by the directive of the authority. For example, if the open-ended directive obligates me to `not murder', I refrain from acting for the reason that the balance of (first order) reasons indicates that I should murder. Thus, we find that `open-ended' directives are no more than a form of conditional directive.

Should the balance of (first order) reasons be, in a particular situation, that I should murder Bob, I then take the open-ended directive "do not murder" as a second-order reason to refrain from acting on this balance of (first order) reasons. In this way, the `open-ended' directive requires action (in this case, *non*-action) when certain conditions are present (the balance of reasons indicates that I should do that which is specified as prohibited).

II. Reconciling Autonomy and Authority

I will argue that, in order for authority to be compatible with autonomy, the obligation to take the authority's directive as authoritative must be imposed through the determination that doing so is the proper way to determine action on the weight of the (first order) reasons. It is this notion that Joseph Raz terms, "The Normal Justification Thesis":

> The normal way to establish that a person has authority over another person involves showing that the alleged subject is likely better to comply with reasons which apply to him (other than the alleged authoritative directives) if he accepts the directives of the alleged authority as authoritatively binding and tries to follow them, rather than by trying to follow the reasons which apply to him directly.[11]

The authority's directive, if it is to be 'de jure' authority at all (which it must be if it is to be other than purely coercive), must derive its normative force from somewhere. I will argue that it derives its normative force from our own evaluation of what should be done, in the manner described by the 'Normal Justification Thesis' (that one is better off complying with the directives of the authority than independently determining what he/she should do).

On this model, in order for the directive of the authority to come to be accepted as binding and obligate compliance on the part of the subject of the directive, the authority's directive must come to be taken as a second order reason for action through the subject's own evaluational judgement. Obedience to this form of authority must be that which one should do on the balance of reasons. We find here a very interesting situation: Obedience to this type of purposive authority requires that the subject make a judgement that what he should do on the balance of reasons is to obey authority. In this way, the justification of authority seems to be an indirect strategy, establishing the directive of the authority as a second-order principle. This leads us directly to the question of whether it remains an indirect strategy, or imposes an obligation on the subject which is independent of the subject's evaluational judgement.

Voluntary Slavery

In justifying authority according to the "Normal Justification Thesis", it is easy to fall into a formal view of autonomy, and attempt to reconcile autonomy and authority through the autonomous determination to appeal to authority. In this, autonomy is compatible with authority so long as the normative obligation to obey authority is derived from the agent's own evaluation that an appeal to authority is the appropriate way to determine action.

However, we have seen that an obligation which is derived from the agent's own evaluational judgement is not necessarily compatible with autonomy. While the autonomous evaluation that one should appeal to authority is a necessary condition for the compatibility of autonomy and authority, the autonomous nature of **this** judgement does not transfer directly to the actual determination of action.

As we saw in the nature of normative obligation generally, there is no transitivity between one's formulation of a principle of action and one's actual determination of action by this principle. Obligations based upon an agent's own evaluational judgement must also be assessed in regard to how the obligation then operates within the agent's practical reasoning. We have seen that there are two fundamentally different ways in which obligations might function within an agent's practical reasoning. Obligations which function as indirect strategies, because they do not threaten the agent's role as "helmsman" in the determination of action, are compatible with the agent's autonomy. However, as imperatives obligations suggest autonomy in that the formulation of the principle of action (the obligation) derives from the agent's own evaluational judgement, but autonomy is then undermined because the agent is then eliminated from the actual determination of action. The obligation assesses relevant reasons for action, and thus acts as "helmsman" in the determination of action.

Let us look at an example of this phenomenon: voluntary slavery. Suppose an agent chooses to become a slave. While it is true that within this role he does not determine what to do, nevertheless he argues that in choosing to be a slave he has determined what to do: be a slave. If the slave has voluntarily entered into slavery, and has determined "being a slave" as the thing to do, can he be said to be autonomous?

This is a difficult question, for it seems that in some sense an agent should perfectly well be able to determine that "being a slave" is the thing to do. After all, the life of a monk in a rigorously disciplined monastery or a marine recruit seem to in many ways closely approximate the life of a slave. Yet, these lifestyles are (in the absence of conscription for the recruit) entered into voluntarily.

In fact, the monk would likely argue that such a lifestyle is *necessary* for his autonomy. To eliminate this option would be to compel him not to do the only thing he could evaluate as the proper thing to do, given his religious convictions. The choice to enter into this lifestyle reflects an evaluation that the only proper thing to do is to devote one's life to God by determining action in a particular way: through reference to the rules of the monastery. Thus, it may be argued that slavery is a strategy for determining action.

Although I will not deny that voluntary slavery is a strategy for determining action, it is akin to the strategy adopted by Kant in formulating action through reference to the categorical imperatives; the strategy operates as an obligation functioning as an imperative within the agent's practical reason. The agent is then eliminated from the practical determination of action.

The voluntary slave does not determine his action. Rather, he only determines that his action will not be determined by himself. While in cases such as the monk's this determination *may* perfectly well be justified, he nonetheless surrenders his autonomy to whatever authority he is obligated to obey.

While it is true that the voluntary slave may "steer" toward slavery, once in slavery the slave is eliminated from the determination of his behavior. To voluntarily enter into slavery is tantamount to placing oneself under the direction of an "automatic pilot"; one may autonomously place oneself in this condition, but cannot be said to "steer" while under this condition.

If autonomy is to be reconciled with authority, the obligation to obey the authority must serve as an indirect strategy rather than as an imperative. In this, the agent must be able to assess his obligation to obey in terms of the normative basis of this obligation. Thus, authority may not be absolute, but must be limited by the normative basis from which it derives its ability to obligate compliance.

The Dependence Thesis

If you will recall the passage discussed earlier (from Raz' Morality of Freedom) involving the arbitrator, you will remember that Raz described the first distinguishing characteristic of that authority as being the fact that the authority's directive (in this case the arbitrator's decision) is not to be taken as a reason to be weighed against other reasons, but rather is to reflect the weighing of those other reasons (and is based upon them). The authority's directive, in this case, replaces the weighing of merits and demerits for particular action by the subject of the directive; the subject accepts the authority's directive as the proper weighing of those (first order) reasons.

In this context, Raz develops what he dubs "The Dependence Thesis". As the nature of an authoritative directive is such that it is meant to reflect a balancing of reasons for action, the normative obligation imposed by a directive is dependent upon its authoritative nature (its being meant to reflect a balance of reasons for action). Limitations on the bindingness of the authority, then, derive from this basis:

> It is not that the arbitrator's word is an absolute reason which has to be obeyed come what may. It can be challenged and justifiably refused in certain circumstances. If, for example, the arbitrator was bribed, or was drunk while considering the case, or if new evidence of great importance unexpectedly turns up, each party may ignore the decision. The point is that reasons that could have been relied upon to justify action before his decision cannot be relied upon once the decision is given.[12]

Raz maintains that the authority's directive is meant to reflect the balance of (first order) reasons for action, and is dependent upon them. Accordingly he requires that the arbitrator not be drunk, or bribed, etc. (her directive thus not reflecting a balance of reasons for action). However, the subject cannot appeal to anything but these types of phenomena to challenge the bindingness of the authority's directive.

If this is the case, it seems that an authority's directive functions as an obligation which circumvents the subject's evaluational judgement. Although Raz offers criteria for undermining an authority's directive, I find these criteria are designed to undermine the directive's applicability, rather than undermining authority on the basis of the agent's evaluational judgement. Let us examine this more closely.

For Raz, the obligation the authority imposes is based upon the fact that the authority's directive is meant to reflect the balance of reasons. It seems the "dependence thesis" only allows the arbitrator's authority to be undermined on the basis of the balance of reasons it is meant to reflect; either new information indicates that the arbitrator's decision was not based upon this new "balance of reasons", or was not meant to reflect a "balance of reasons" at all (e.g. a bribe). Even then, it is not the fact that the arbitrator's decision does not reflect the balance of reasons that undermines his authority, but the fact that the decision did not attempt to determine the balance of reasons:

> Notice that a dependent reason is not one which does in fact reflect the balance of reasons on which it depends: it is one which is meant to do so.[13]

In this way, Raz only allows one to undermine authority on the basis of its applicability. So long as the arbitrator's decision *was meant to* reflect the balance of reasons upon which it depends, it is binding. To undermine authority, one would need to show that the decision was not meant to reflect a balance of reasons (the arbitrator was bribed, etc.). This is tantamount to undermining the obligation to comply by showing that this is not an authoritative decision (an *authoritative* decision is meant to reflect the balance of first order reasons upon which it depends). Thus, so long as it is authoritative, the agent's practical judgement cannot affect the determination of action.

An authoritative directive whose bindingness is undermined in this way amounts to a second-order reason functioning as an imperative. The obligation to comply can only be undermined by reference to the fact that this is not an *authoritative* directive (it is not meant to reflect the balance of first order reasons upon which it depends). If the directive is authoritative, it eliminates the agent's evaluational judgement from the determination of action.

The Dependence Thesis Revised

Where I think Raz went wrong is in attempting to maintain that the authority's directive is undermined through its dependence on the balance of (first order) reasons it is meant to reflect. Raz does not need to maintain this in order to recognize the limitations he wishes upon authoritative directives. In fact, I will argue that it is more consistent with Raz' theory of authority (in terms of content-independent obligation) to maintain that the directive does not need to be meant to reflect a balance of (first order) reasons for action, but rather needs to reflect the reason(s) one has for appealing to authority.

In this case, the foundation of authority is again the evaluation by the subject that the weighing of merits and demerits for action should be determined by the authority, rather than weighed himself. Similarly, this same evaluation is what serves to undermine the authority. I will argue that the purposive nature of such authority provides a ground upon which the subject must evaluate the very directive of the authority, regardless of its 'content independent' imposition of obligation. If the authority's directive fails to reflect those things for which one appeals to authority, then it fails to impose an obligation to obey.[14]

Let us examine this more closely, using the model of second order reasoning within which we have been working. On the intuitive model of practical reason and action[15], one should do that which is indicated by the balance of reasons. This is a direct determination of what one's action should be. The second order reason provided by the presence of a binding authoritative directive is meant to preempt such a weighing of the balance of reasons for action. It does **not**, however, preempt a weighing of the balance of reasons *to take the authority's utterance as a second order reason for action*.

Whereas the balance of reasons for action inherent in the intuitive model of practical reason and action is concerned with the determination of what action one should engage in, the reasons for taking a second order reason for action are concerned with the determination of *how* one should determine the proper 'reason for action'. This is important, because when I discuss the 'reasons for taking the authority's directive as a second order reason for action', this does not change the content-independent nature of the authority's directive. Although the content of the authority's directive *does* affect the balance of reasons for taking the directive as a second order reason for action, this is not the same as the balance of reasons the directive (if taken as a second order reason for action) is meant to replace in a content-independent fashion. The content of the directive affects only the balance of reasons for taking the authority's directive as a second order (content-independent) reason for action.

The second order reason derives its normative force from the fact that the 'balance of (first order) reasons' indicates that one should **not** determine (directly) what one's actions should be by weighing the balance of (first order) reasons. Rather, it indicates that one should take the authority's evaluation of the balance of reasons as content-independently binding. It also requires that, once the directive is issued, the balance of reasons continues to indicate one should take the authority's evaluation as binding. In this way, the authority's directive can be viewed as a second order reason functioning as an indirect strategy toward an end the subject sets for himself.

On Raz' version of the dependence thesis, the authority's normative force was dependent on the authority's decision being meant to reflect the balance of first-order reasons for action (the very balance of reasons it is meant to replace). On my version of the dependence thesis, the authority's normative force is dependent on the reason(s) for which one appealed to the authority.

Shifting the focus of the dependence thesis away from the balance of reasons which the authority's decision is meant to replace, to the reason(s) for which one appeals to authority, not only shifts the obligation from the form of a second-order reason functioning as an imperative to that of an indirect strategy; it more consistently recognizes the content-independent nature of an authoritative directive. If the normative force of an authoritative directive is dependent on its being meant to reflect some balance of (first-order) reasons, the legitimate content of an authoritative directive is quite restricted. On the other hand, if the normative force of the authoritative directive is dependent on the reason(s) for which one appeals to the authority, the directive may have any content whatsoever so long as the directive does not undermine the very reason for which one appeals to authority.

To illustrate this point, let us consider a Hobbesian sovereign. On Raz' version of the dependence thesis, it would seem that the sovereign would have to issue directives that are *meant* to reflect the balance of reasons, etc. If the sovereign makes arbitrary decisions, they are invalid. But this seems to miss the point of the Hobbesian sovereign. We appeal to the sovereign in order to avoid the evils of the state of nature; *any* authority is better than the state of nature. This is our reason for appealing to the sovereign. He can make arbitrary decisions, etc. as much as he wants (we hope he is more responsible, but have no guarantee), and we are still obligated to comply. So long as his directives do not fail to take us out of the state of nature (and in this way fail to reflect the reason for which we appealed to the sovereign), the directives are authoritative. It is this limitation which my version of the dependence thesis places on the sovereign.

The Limits of Authority

Let us look at an example of this type of authority. I am feeling very ill, and would like to relieve the pain I experience as a result of my illness. I could begin to attempt to weigh the pros and cons of various remedies, but this will be hit-and-miss at best, since I have no medical training. Likewise, to engage in various remedies on the basis of my strongest impulse might be creative, but it is unlikely to accomplish the end I would really like (to relieve pain). Therefore, I go to a doctor. I take the doctor's evaluation as authoritative; I will not simply throw his advice into the pool of reasons for action. I no longer attempt to make independent judgments as to what remedy I should try. I take the physician's order as a reason for action *independent of its content, and of my own evaluation of what should be done*.[16]

The authority's normative force is derived from my ignorance of medicine, coupled with his expertise. I may evaluate the directive upon the basis of my reason to go to a doctor (his medical expertise) to determine if his directive reflects this reason (If he is drunk, I might decide that his opinion does not reflect his medical expertise, and so not take his directives as authoritative.), but I do not evaluate the content of the doctor's directive per se (I do not evaluate, on the basis of the content of the directive, whether it reflects a weighing of first order reasons,[17] for it is my inability to make such evaluations which provides the purpose for appealing to authority).

The presence of the 'reason' to obey authority is also quite important. There are parameters not only to knowledge, but also to lack of knowledge. While I may recognize my lack of medical knowledge, along with the physician's expertise in medicine, as a reason to take the physician's order as authoritative, I also recognize the limits of acceptable authoritative directives by the physician. I do this in two ways. The first is very simple. If I go to the physician to find the best way to relieve pain, I will not accept, as authoritative, directives by the physician which fall outside the domain for which I went to the physician. For instance, I will not accept as authoritative the physician's directive that 'Wheel of Fortune' is not worth watching, and that I should not watch it.

The second way I recognize limits to the acceptability of an authority's directives is through a general norm of acceptable ranges. What do I mean by this? I mean that we may expect, for example, that the physician will tell us to "take two aspirin and call me in the morning". Such a statement by the physician may very well be taken as authoritative. However, if the physician were to say, "take 46,000 pills an hour for the next ten years", we would more than likely not accept this as authoritative. Why? Because there is an end which we wish to achieve in going to the physician. We expect that his prescription will help us to achieve this end. If we do not think that following the prescription will achieve this, we likely will not take it as authoritative.

Because the subject appealed to the authority for the reason (as indicated by the normal justification thesis) that what we should do is what is indicated by the 'balance of reasons', and this indicates that we should take the physician's advice as authoritative, the failure of the directive to facilitate the expectation that this end will be fulfilled changes the normative situation once again. Where before we felt that the balance of reasons was best determined by the authority, and so felt obligated to obey, this normative obligation is no longer present when the balance of reasons no longer indicates that one should take a directive as authoritative[18]. This feature is key; for it confirms that such purposive authority is, in fact, an indirect strategy rather than an obligation which circumvents the evaluational judgement of the subject.

The implications of the above analysis of authority are quite interesting. Although the subject does not determine the content of the authority's directive, the subject *does* determine that the appropriate way to weigh the reasons for action is through appeal to the authority. In this way, the normative force of the authority's directive is derived from the subject's own evaluational judgement that what he/she should do is to take the directive as authoritative (the subject sets his own end). In addition, the subject evaluates the directive's content to determine if the directive reflects the reason the agent had for taking it as authoritative (the subject continues to steer).

The appeal to such (purposive) authority is in essence an indirect strategy. The end is set by the subject himself, and the subject continues to steer in that the subject must evaluate whether the indirect strategy will achieve the end he wishes. Thus, the problems we encountered with the voluntary slave are not present, as the subject himself sets the end, and continues to steer in evaluating the content of the directive in terms of the reasons for appealing to authority. Furthermore, this indirect strategy **is** authoritative. One surrenders one's own evaluation of 'the balance of reasons' to that of the authority. Thus, the authority's directive remains *in this sense* content-independent.

---

[1] See Wolff, Robert Paul In Defense of Anarchism (New York: Harper and Row, 1970).

[2] Raz, The Morality of Freedom (New York: Oxford University Press, 1986) p.24.

[3] Raz, The Morality of Freedom, pp.25-26.

[4] Raz, The Morality of Freedom, pp.41-42.

[5] Hart, H.L.A., Essays on Bentham, (Oxford: Clarendon Press, 1982), p.254. A content independent reason is a reason for action regardless of what is called for.

[6] Child, James W. "Specific Commands, General Rules and Degrees of Autonomy", unpublished paper. A modified version of this paper has subsequently been published in The Canadian Journal of Law and Juris Prudence, Volume VIII, No. 2 (July, 1995).

[7] Child, "Specific Commands, General Rules and Degrees of Autonomy", p.1.

[8] Child, "Specific Commands, General Rules and Degrees of Autonomy", p.2-3.

[9] Child, "Specific Commands, General Rules and Degrees of Autonomy", p.8-9.

[10] Of course, I could kill Old Joe. But that would not influence how I judge whether Old Joe is dead; rather, it only influences the conditions to which I apply the judgement.

[11] Raz, The Morality of Freedom, p.53.

[12] Raz, The Morality of Freedom, p.42.

[13] Raz, The Morality of Freedom, p.41.

¹⁴I will show that this does not, however, affect the 'content-independent' nature of the authority's directive.

¹⁵Raz, Joseph, "Reasons for Actions, Decisions and Norms" in Raz, Joseph (ed.) Practical Reasoning (New York: Oxford University Press, 1978) p.130.

¹⁶There are many times when we accept a directive as a very weighty reason to do something. But, unless this replaces our own evaluation, rather than simply affecting our own evaluation, the person who utters this does not exercise authority over us. He simply attempts to affect our evaluation, rather than replace it.

¹⁷There is an exception to this, which I will discuss in a few pages. This exception consists of a situation in which the doctor's order is so outlandish that, even though I am not trained in medicine, I know the order does not reflect medical training. In such a case, I evaluate the content, but from the perspective that such an order indicates the doctor is not currently making judgments which reflect the reasons I went to him (his medical expertise). Even in such a case, however, I do not independently determine the best action. I merely determine that the appropriate way to determine action is not by appeal to this doctor.

¹⁸This model of authority is one which I feel is soundly grounded in the normative force of the 'intuitive model of practical reason and action'. While this grounding does not require that the 'intuitive model' be complete, my model of normative obligation and obedience to authority derives normative force to the degree that one assigns any normative force at all to the intuitive model that one ought to do that which is indicated by the balance of reasons (in this abstract form).

CHAPTER SEVEN
Autonomy and the Authority of Law

Thus far, we have examined individual autonomy and how it is effected by external considerations. In doing so, we have seen that autonomy is not only compatible with a variety of external influences on the determination of action, but is even compatible with certain forms of authority (the implication being that it is the model of authority which is compatible with autonomy that we should recognize). We shall now turn our attention to a specific form of authority - that which society exercises over its citizens. This form of authority has interested man for centuries in the form of questions concerning the relation of the individual to society, of freedom and authority, and of individual vs. social goods.

Throughout this work, I have maintained that a viable conception of autonomy must allow for appeals to various forms of authority. Foremost among these is the authority which structures and organizes interaction between people living together in society. Most commonly, this authority takes the form of a legal system. The authority of a legal system, and the obligation imposed by the particular laws which are its directives, is vital at a practical level if we are to attain the goods which we value from living in society.

Thomas Hobbes described life devoid of societal authority as a "state of nature", and graphically conveyed the problems which might arise from such a state. War of all against all, and the precarious nature of survival are accentuated through the fatal threat which even the weakest among us pose to even those most capable of defending themselves. Life in such a state would be "solitary, poor, nasty, brutish and short".

While Hobbes' description of the state of nature is surely a worst-case scenario, contestable in its extreme portrayal of the hardships of such a state, even much less harsh portrayals of a state of nature offer a far less attractive picture of life than that offered by "civilized" society. Though in practice the violent war of all against all would probably be far more limited than Hobbes would have us believe, it would still likely be far more pervasive than in a society subject to rules of conduct. For one, the ability to seek recourse to such violence would certainly be less available.

Living in a society subject to authoritative rules of conduct provides security from violence, even if this security is not perfect. Recourse toward those who violate the standards of conduct is provided to all, not just those who are able to mount this on their own behalf. In addition, the violation of the rules of conduct provides a ground for social criticism (and punishment) which is simply not available in society devoid of these rules of conduct. In short, a society subject to authoritative rules of conduct at the very least establishes the conditions in which security from violence might be attained. But as we shall see below, this security can only be accomplished if the rules of conduct are not followed informally, allowing subjects to constantly balance conformity with the gains of violating the standards. The rules must pre-empt this balancing if we are to feel secure. That is, the rules must be *authoritative*.

In addition to security from violence, life in a society subject to rules of conduct allows people living in that society to attain positive goods which would be unattainable in a society devoid of such rules. This is true in two respects. First, the rules of conduct established by society provides people with a stable environment in which to pursue projects. F.A. Hayek describes law as follows:

> The law tells (an individual) what facts he may count on and thereby extends the range within which he can predict the consequences of his actions...the law thus serves to enable the individual to act effectively on his own knowledge.[1]

This stability can only be provided to the extent that we can count on others to conform to the rules. As we shall see below, this again requires that the law be *authoritative*.

Secondly, the rules of society allow people to attain goods through cooperative action. These cooperative actions require that people disarm themselves in a variety of ways, and be able to *trust* others to reciprocate. By establishing *authoritative* rules which facilitate this trust, society enables individuals to broaden the range of projects which they might only undertake through cooperation with others.

By providing conditions in which people may "drop their guard" secure from violence to pursue projects other than mere survival, by providing the conditions of stability in which people can viably pursue projects and act effectively on plans, and by providing the conditions under which cooperative projects may be undertaken, the authoritative rules of society enhance the autonomy of people living in that society. These "goods", however, can only be supplied if the rules of society are *authoritative*. Societal authority, then, is perhaps the most important form of authority which a viable conception of autonomy must allow for. Let us now examine how societal authority might be compatible with autonomy on the model I have outlined.

The first task which faces us in examining the effect of societal authority on individual autonomy is to establish the type of obligation which society places upon us. Can societal authority legitimately be described as imposing the type of obligation which is compatible with autonomy, or does society place obligations upon us which then take on a life of their own, supersede the agent's evaluational judgement, and thus are not compatible with autonomy? To answer this question, we shall examine what I take to be the paradigm form of societal obligation - the obligation to obey the law.

The first step in our examination of the obligation to obey the law is to establish the nature of such an obligation. We shall undertake this project in the context of Joseph Raz's model of the authority of law. We shall do this for several reasons. First, Raz provides *the* leading analysis of legal systems in terms of reasons for action. More importantly, however, the model of authority we have developed in the preceding chapter draws heavily upon Raz's analysis of authority, and certain changes we have made to that model (particularly to the "dependence thesis"). The terminology, then, should easily translate. Finally, by applying the model of authority we have developed to Raz's own analysis of the authority of law, the importance of the revisions we have made to Raz's model of authority should become clear: the revisions provide grounds which enable us to reverse Raz's position on whether the obligation to obey the law is justified.

We shall view the legal system as a form of (social) authority, justified by reference to the goods we attain through life in a rule-governed society. The particular laws which constitute this authority's directives, however, must be consistent with the reasons which justified our adopting this authority. In this way, we shall see that the authority of law is not only justified, but operates as the type of authority which is consistent with the autonomy of its subjects (as described in the previous chapter).

Over several works[2], Raz examines the concept of authority and a variety of arguments for why a subject to a legal system might have reasons to comply with its demands. Raz concludes that these arguments fail to justify the authority of law for most people. Furthermore, he argues that because of the conceptual nature of law's claim to content-independent appeal for compliance, it is unlikely that the authority of a legal system could be justified for more than a small portion of society. As we shall see below, Raz's position stems from the fact that law claims an appeal for content-independent compliance, by *all* subjects, to *all* laws, at *all* times (unless the law *itself* identifies exceptions).

I will argue that Raz's conclusions concerning the reasons subjects have (or, for Raz, lack) to comply with the directives of a legal system are tied to a specific feature of his model of reasons for action and authority. Specifically, his conclusions are tied to his formulation of the "dependence thesis" (which we shall examine in detail below). However, Raz's formulation of this thesis focuses on the wrong set of "reasons" which apply to the subject. Namely, it focuses on the "reasons for action" which the directives of a legal system is meant to replace, rather than the reasons the subject has to appeal to the legal system. When the dependence thesis is revised according to this distinction, it becomes clear how an agent has reasons to comply with the legal system, though she might not have reasons to comply with certain specific laws within that legal system.

Most interestingly, this model of reasons for action and authority is perfectly consistent with our conceptual understanding of authority as obligating compliance in a content-independent manner. Indeed, I shall argue that this revised understanding of the dependence thesis is more consistent with the content-independent nature of an obligation to comply with authority than Raz's original formulation.

On the Obligation to Obey the Law

There are two fundamental approaches we might take concerning the obligation to obey the law. The first holds that the obligation to obey is a "general" obligation to obey the legal system. This approach obligates one to obey the law *because the law demands it*, and thus the obligation to obey does not hinge in any way upon the content of a specific law (which might be called into question). If it is required by law, one is obligated to comply. If one questions the "rightness" of a specific law, one might attempt to have that law changed. But the obligation to obey holds at a general level, and so until this specific law in fact changes, one remains obligated to comply.

The second approach to the obligation to obey the law holds that the obligation to obey is a *prima facie* obligation, and as such is subject to review case-by-case. This approach allows the specific content of certain laws to call into question the obligation to comply. While the *prima facie* obligation to comply places the burden of argument upon the person who would maintain there is no obligation to comply, it does allow that some laws should not obligate compliance on the part of some people. It also allows that laws which are not "right" might not obligate compliance, even if these laws remain on the books.

The strength of the first approach is that it captures the conceptual character of "binding" law. Because the obligation to obey is not subject to case-by-case review, it obligates compliance to the law *because it is the law*, and does not attach the obligation to obey to the specific circumstances or content of law. In this, a "general" obligation to obey the law can establish an obligation to obey the law *qua* law which an obligation that is subject to case-by-case review cannot.

If the obligation to obey is established in each case only after considering the merits and demerits of obedience, it is difficult to imagine how the law *qua* law contributes to an obligation to obey. It seems that it is the merits and demerits of obedience in each case which impose the obligation (or lack thereof) to obey. This would undermine the very reasons we have for adopting a legal system. As Chaim Gans has recently pointed out, the advantage the law offers is the "concretization of the reasons on which we should act"[3], and this requires that the law provides reasons for our actions *because it is the law*, above the reasons that apply to our actions independently. For example, there may be very good independent reasons (reasons independent of the fact that the law requires it) for me not to murder my companion to the movies. But the obligation to obey the law requires that we not murder our companion even if these independent reasons do not hold (indeed, even if I have a reason to kill him), *because it is forbidden by law*. In this way, the obligation imposed by law does not appear to be subject to assessment on a case-by-case basis.

It is this concern with the authority of law *qua* law which leads Joseph Raz to reject the possibility of a *prima facie* obligation to obey the law.[4] The problems Raz sees with an obligation to obey which is *prima facie* can be traced to his model of obligation to authority, in which the only "trump" over the obligation to obey is described in what he calls "The Dependence Thesis".[5] Here, Raz describes the directives of an authority as obligating compliance so long as the directive is meant to reflect the "balance of reasons which it is meant to replace".

On the Razian view of authority, authority obligates compliance because "...The alleged subject is likely better to comply with reasons which apply to him (other than the alleged authoritative directives) if he accepts the directives of the alleged authority as authoritatively binding and tries to follow them, rather than by trying to follow the reasons which apply to him directly."[6] Raz dubs this "The Normal Justification Thesis". The dependence thesis stems from this justification of authority: the authoritative nature of the directive depends upon its being meant to reflect the reasons which (on the normal justification thesis) we are better off appealing to the authority to balance than acting on our own attempts to balance. So long as the authority's directive is *meant* to reflect the reasons which apply to the subject independently, these reasons cannot be used to question the directive of the authority, because the very reason we appeal to authority (on the normal justification thesis) is that the reasons which apply independently are more likely to be complied with if we follow the directives of the authority, rather than acting on our own determination of what these reasons require.

On the other hand, to eliminate the possibility of a *real* check on the content of law imposes an obligation to obey which is far too strong. There are times when we feel people should *not* obey the law, and times when we even feel that people should *disobey* the law. A plethora of examples of this attitude can be found by examining our reactions to the laws of Nazi Germany concerning Jews, or laws in the deep south of the United States in the 1950s concerning Black people. A strong general obligation to obey the law cannot provide *real* checks on the content of such laws through their questionable *content*. The characteristic feature of such an obligation is that it is *content-independent*.[7]

For example, consider Raz's position on the binding nature of an authority's directive. The only check on authority is provided by what Raz dubs "The Dependence Thesis". As the nature of an authoritative directive is such that it is meant to reflect a balancing of reasons for action, the normative obligation imposed by a directive is dependent upon its authoritative nature (its being meant to reflect a balance of reasons for action). Limitations on the bindingness of the authority, then, derive from this basis:

> It is not that the arbitrator's word is an absolute reason which has to be obeyed come what may. It can be challenged and justifiably refused in certain circumstances. If, for example, the arbitrator was bribed, or was drunk while considering the case, or if new evidence of great importance unexpectedly turns up, each party may ignore the decision. The point is that reasons that could have been relied upon to justify action before his decision cannot be relied upon once the decision is given.[8]

One can see here the elimination of the seemingly absurd evaluation of the authority's directive on the basis of an assessment of the very reasons we acknowledge are better assessed by the authority when we appeal to authority. This absurd position is avoided because the "reasons that could have been relied upon to justify action before his decision cannot be relied upon once the decision is made". The "check" that Raz offers in its place is based solely upon the authority's *attempt* to assess the reasons we appeal to him to assess. Raz maintains that the authority's directive is meant to reflect the balance of reasons for action, and is dependent upon them. Accordingly he requires that the arbitrator not be drunk, or bribed, etc. (her directive thus not reflecting a balance of reasons for action). But the *content* of the law per se cannot call the legitimacy of the law into question; the only thing which can call the legitimacy of the law into question is whether the law is *meant to* reflect the "balance of reasons upon which it depends".

Because the content-independent nature of law is so general, Raz believes it will be difficult to justify an obligation to obey for more than a few people. The reasons for this are varied, but as we shall see below, most center around the fact that the law claims an appeal for compliance by all people, to all laws, at all times. To have reasons to appeal to such a strong form of authority unlikely. Let us examine Raz's arguments.

Arguments Against an Obligation to Obey the Law

In a book entitled The Authority of Law, Raz examines and rejects what he takes to be the strongest arguments for the existence of an obligation to obey the law. Rather than positively establishing the non-existence of a general duty to obey the law, Raz undertakes the project of rejecting arguments that such a duty exists, by showing that none of the arguments given for the obligation to obey the law succeed in justifying the strong content-independent obligation which the law claims..

The first of these is the argument that disobedience sets a bad example, and inclines other people to break the law.[9] We shall refer to this as the 'bad example' argument. Raz sites the example of the Archbishop of Canterbury, whose position in society significantly influences the attitudes and practices of many people. Thus, for the Archbishop of Canterbury to disobey the law might influence the attitude of many people toward the law, and foster a general disrespect.

While Raz recognizes the importance of this argument ("Though most of us cannot influence public attitudes in the way the Archbishop of Canterbury can, we do affect other people's attitudes even if in smaller measure"[10]), he questions its significance in establishing an *obligation* to obey the law. At best, Raz maintains, the 'bad example' argument provides a prima facie reason to obey the law, not a "Pre-eminent reason amounting to an obligation."[11] Raz sites examples of disobedience which actually strengthen general obedience, or encourage disobedience only to very bad laws.[12] In addition, many offenses are never detected (and it can be known in advance that they will never be detected)[13], and so cannot provide a bad example. Thus, the obligation to obey the law, if grounded in the 'bad example' argument, would not be able to adequately cover these cases.

The second argument for an obligation to obey the law is grounded in promising: by living in a society one promises (either explicitly or implicitly) to obey that society's laws. However, Raz finds this argument inadequate as well. Since the normative force of promising and other voluntary commitments is created by an *expressed intention* to be bound[14], an implicit commitment is inadequate to ground a general obligation to obey the law (past obedience, for example, cannot itself imply a commitment to be bound). Most *explicit* promises to obey the law (e.g. an oath of allegiance, etc.) are given in conditions of coercion or duress[15], and those cases in which it is not (e.g. voluntarily assuming an office of state to which an oath of allegiance is attached) are the exception rather than the rule. Most people simply do not explicitly commit themselves to obey the law.[16]

The third argument for an obligation to obey the law is based upon the expectations of others, and their reliance upon the predictability of obedience. Raz presents this argument as follows:

> If by his behaviour a person knowingly induces another to rely on him then he should not, other things being equal, frustrate the expectations of that other person if doing so affects him adversely. Thus if, for example, I knowingly induce another to obey the law by words or actions which lead him to believe that I will obey the law myself, then I should, other things being equal, not let him down by breaking the law.[17]

This argument, however, only applies if I adversely affect the man who relied upon me. Raz argues that disobedience does not always affect anybody[18], and that it is rare that people *knowingly* induce the kind of reliance in others which would lead to this adverse affect:

> Even if it is true that one's behaviour induces others to obey the law, it is certainly not something that people are normally aware of. Most people do not believe that others obey the law because they expect them to do so.[19]

That one *knowingly* induces the reliance which results in an adverse affect is vital, as Raz illustrates in the following counter-example:

> It is true that up to a point, and especially in certain areas of the law, people are encouraged to obey by the expectation that others will generally do likewise. But this is no more a reason for me to obey than the fact that many Londoners are encouraged to remain in London by the expectation that many people will continue to live there is a reason against any person leaving the city.[20]

Thus, the argument from reliance is not adequate to ground the type of obligation which the law claims.

The fourth argument for an obligation to obey the law is based upon consent, and is taken by Raz from Peter Singer's Democracy and Disobedience.[21] Laws established by democratic procedures imply the consent of the subjects. In voting, one is implying consent to the majority decision.[22] Raz dismisses this argument quickly on the basis that Singer makes a false factual assumption that participation implies consent to a majority decision procedure: "People generally know that non-democrats do participate in democratic elections".[23]

Singer also offers an argument that democracy provides a fair compromise procedure, and that one has a reason to accept its results as fair. This argument, however, relies on a duty to support just institutions[24], and Raz shows that the duty to support just institutions is insufficient to establish an obligation to obey the law.[25] That a law is established by a procedure one accepts does not mean one accepts the law itself. As Raz states concerning the democratic decision procedure:

> One may approve of it as expressing trust in the mature judgement of the population...and yet not acknowledge that each one of its decisions ought to be obeyed just because it was democratically reached.[26]

Finally, Raz examines prudential reasons that people may have for adopting an obligation to obey the law. To assess in each case whether a law should be obeyed would incur great costs in time, effort, and calculation.[27] In addition, because we live in an imperfect world, we are likely to make mistakes in judgement. Thus, one might adopt a policy of always obeying the law rather than determining in each case whether one should obey that law.

One can see in the above argument a strategy very much like that of Ann in the example of second-order reasoning discussed in chapter five. Just as Ann adopted a policy of 'not deciding' because she did not trust her own judgement, the above argument adopts a policy of not determining for each law whether one ought to obey because of the time, effort and other costs involved. In this way, the above argument for 'general obedience' looks (at first glance) like an indirect strategy.

However, recall that in the case of Ann, the policy to 'not decide' was subject to review upon the basis of the reasons for which the policy was adopted. It is this which is vital for autonomy, for the agent's own evaluational judgement retains the ability to assess the policy (and whether it should apply). While we may often assess the reasons for adopting the policy of obedience as best most of the time, it surely is not the case that we would always adopt this policy. As Raz states:

> So far as prudence is concerned, almost everyone, though he has reason to follow a conformist policy in most areas, is free to exempt certain very low-risk areas from them: minor offenses against the property of one's employer, minor violations of tax law, etc.[28]

Prudence would seem to indicate that we not adopt an all-embracing general obligation to obey the law, but retain the ability to not adopt this policy in those cases where the costs of case-by-case assessment are not greater than the benefits. Thus, an indirect strategy of this sort will not establish a general obligation to obey the law, even though it may establish a policy of obedience in some areas (which may be "trumped" by the agent's assessment that the costs do not warrant adopting such a policy).

As we have seen, Raz dislikes the idea of approaching the obligation to obey the law as prima facie, believing that the obligation to obey the law is much more stringent.[29] The obligation to obey the law, for Raz, must be a content-independent obligation and so cannot be a prima facie obligation.

Although Raz rejects the notion of a prima facie obligation to obey the law, I will not dismiss this approach so readily. The reasons for this are twofold. First, as I shall argue below, an understanding of the obligation to obey the law as prima facie in the ways I shall characterize better captures the nature of law as content-independently binding on the revised understanding of the dependence thesis (developed in the preceding chapter). Secondly, if we are to make autonomy and the authority of law compatible, the obligation to obey the law must be prima facie in the way that obligations functioning as indirect strategies are "trumped" by an agent's evaluational judgement.

It would be useful here to recall our examination of the way in which obligations function within practical reasoning. There, in order for an obligation to be consistent with an agent's autonomy, the obligation must serve as the type of second-order reason which we called an 'indirect strategy'. This required that the obligation be subject to the agent's continued assessment by way of the reasons which formed the basis upon which the obligation was established. In this, the obligation was subject to review in each case to determine whether the obligation reflected the reasons for which the obligation was established.

The obligation to obey the law, then, must be subject to continued assessment by the subject if it is to remain compatible with autonomy. To fail to subject each case to review and establish a general obligation to obey the law would be tantamount to establishing the obligation to obey the law as the type of second-order reason which functions as an imperative.[30] In this, the obligation to obey the law would be inconsistent with autonomy in the same way that voluntary slavery was found to be inconsistent with autonomy in the previous chapter. Since there is no transitivity between autonomously adopting some decision procedure (such as slavery or obedience to the law) and the autonomy of the agent when determining actions within that decision procedure, a "general" obligation to obey the law cannot establish the compatibility of autonomy and the obligation to obey the law, for a "general" obligation to obey the law is established in the abstract, and "trumps" case-by-case assessments of whether there is an obligation to obey.

As we shall see below, I believe Raz' problems with the prima facie character of the authority of law can be traced to his model of obligation to authority, in which the only "trump" over this obligation is described in the dependence thesis. By making the same adjustments we made to Raz' dependence thesis in the previous chapter, we can establish an obligation to obey the law which is subject to review by the agent, yet retains its content-independent character (just as in the previous chapter we were able to make the obligation to obey authority subject to such review while retaining its content-independent character).

The Debate in Context

A prima facie obligation to obey the law must be subject to certain "checks" which might override the obligation. This seems incompatible with the notion of content-independent obligation which Raz has formulated. For Raz, the "check" upon authority provided by the dependence thesis is not really a "check" so much as it is a test of "proper pedigree". The obligation the authority imposes is based upon the fact that the authority's directive is meant to reflect the balance of reasons which apply independently. The Dependence Thesis allows the subject to appeal the authority's decision only when the subject can show that the authority's decision did not reflect this balance; Either new information indicates that the arbitrator's decision was not based upon this new "balance of reasons", or it can be shown that the decision was not meant to reflect the "balance of reasons" at all (e.g. a bribe). Even then, it is not the fact that the arbitrator's decision does not reflect the balance of reasons that undermines his authority, but the fact that the decision did not attempt to determine the balance of reasons:

> Notice that a dependent reason is not one which does in fact reflect the balance of reasons on which it depends: it is one which is meant to do so.[31]

So long as the arbitrator's decision *was meant to* reflect the balance of reasons upon which it depends, it is binding. To undermine authority, one would need to show that the decision was not meant to reflect a balance of reasons (the arbitrator was bribed, etc.). This is tantamount to undermining the obligation to comply by showing that this is simply not an authoritative decision, because an **authoritative** decision is meant to reflect the balance of reasons upon which it depends.

Thus, we are left with only one question in regard to whether we should comply with the directives of authority: "Is this in fact an *authoritative* directive?". In the context of law, this question becomes "Is this in fact a *legal* requirement?". In our society, a *legal* requirement is one which reflects the balance of interests as determined by the vote of our representatives in Congress (given certain Constitutional limitations in the United States, but not in Great Britain). If the law is meant to reflect the vote of Congress, it is properly law. In this, the question posed by the dependence thesis is simply one of "Is this law *meant to reflect proper pedigree?*" (this is the Positivist element of Raz's theory of law). If the answer is yes, one is obligated to comply whatever the content of the law. If the answer is no, it is not a legal requirement at all and so the question of compliance does not arise (at least in the context of the obligation to obey the law). From the above, we can see that the check Raz provides on the binding nature of law is nothing more than a "Positivist" question of pedigree. This will not allow for disobedience to "wrong" or immoral laws which do pass proper pedigree, like the laws of Nazi Germany for example, and so cannot capture our belief that such laws should not be obeyed (we shall discuss this in greater detail below).

We are left, then, with a traditional "Legal Positivism / Natural Law" debate concerning the obligation to obey the law. The Positivist, like Raz, believes that conceptually, the binding character of law cannot be sacrificed for the sake of our intuitions against laws like those of Nazi Germany. The Natural Law theorist believes the moral repugnance of laws like those of Nazi Germany are too high a price to pay for a strong obligation to obey. The debate concerning the obligation to obey the law seems to cash out at this point, and bog down in the perennial debate between these schools of thought.

However, the debate need not, and indeed *should not*, stop here. The strength of each school is that it seems to capture an element of law we hold dear: The Positivist camp provides a strong obligation to obey; The Natural Law camp captures our intuitions that law should be at least consistent with morality. The major drawback of each school is that it seems incompatible with the strength of the other. I shall argue below that this last point is not the case. If we adopt a two-level model of the obligation to obey the law, we can capture the strengths of both the Positivist and Natural Law camps, in a way which is coherent and logically consistent.

A Two-Level Model of the Obligation to Obey the Law

The purpose of a legal system is to secure conformity in certain cooperative areas of life, particularly those areas in which we interact with others in society. Certain goods can only be achieved through social interaction. This interaction requires that we "trust" others to cooperate in joint ventures, even if these "joint ventures" only consist in the observance of certain standards of conduct (such as not engaging in behavior which might place others in significant danger). For these joint ventures to be viable, we need assurances that others will cooperate in the venture, otherwise we disadvantage ourselves in vain.

The advantage law offers is that it makes it more likely that these cooperative ventures will not be in vain, and in this makes social goods achievable, and *rational*. For example, Chaim Gans uses the payment of taxes. In order for us to have a reason to pay taxes we must believe that certain advantages will result. For this to happen, we must be assured that enough other people will also pay their taxes. The law provides this guarantee. States Gans:

> When the legal authority commands us to pay taxes, then, it helps us to do what we should, not by informing us about an act of which we weren't aware, but by creating the conditions under which there is reason for doing what we knew anyway that we should do.[32]

The purpose of law is to promote certain structures of interaction between people, and in this way facilitate the goods which can be achieved only through living in society. The way in which the law facilitates these goods is by providing a "concrete" set of rules which we can count on others to observe.[33]

Let us stop here to consider why Raz is so adamantly against the idea of a prima facie obligation to obey the law. For Raz, the obligation to obey authority must be content-independent. This means that the obligation to obey is not contingent upon the specific content of the authority's directive. If the content of each particular law might call into question its ability to obligate compliance, our ability to count on others to observe particular laws is significantly weakened. For example, consider the laws regulating traffic. We need to be able to count on others to drive on a consistent side of the road. If each other driver is entitled to constantly assess their obligation to drive on a particular side, the "good" achieved through traffic law is undermined. Likewise, the safety we gain from living in a society governed by laws is undermined if people retain the ability to constantly assess their reasons not to kill us. The function of law can only be achieved if we can count on a general observation of laws by the general population.[34] Thus, Raz establishes qualifications upon the obligation to obey authority only through the dependence thesis. As we have seen, the dependence thesis supports a "strong" obligation to obey laws which pass the test of "proper pedigree"; If this test is passed, law is content-independently binding.

Recall that the dependence thesis was derived from what Raz dubbed "The Normal Justification Thesis". This stated that the normal way one establishes an obligation to obey authority is to show that the subject is more likely to comply with reasons which apply to him independently if he obeys authority. The dependence thesis then requires that the authority's directive be meant to reflect these reasons which apply to the subject independently if the subject is to be obligated to obey.

We saw above how Raz's version of the dependence thesis does not really serve as a limitation on authority so much as it serves as a test for *authoritative* obligation. To fail the dependence thesis (to issue a directive which is not meant to reflect the reasons which apply to the subject independently) does not override or undermine the obligation to obey authority, but rather serves to establish that this directive is not an **authoritative** directive, and thus does not obligate obedience. For Raz, then, the only test by which to qualify the obligation to obey authority involves establishing that the authority's directive is not actually authoritative, and thus no obligation to obey exists. Disobedience based upon the dependence thesis, then, would not be prima facie wrong, as there would exist **no** obligation to obey.

Raz, then, must be against the idea of a prima facie obligation to obey the law. A law is either authoritative or it is not. The only legitimate assessment of a law is the dependence thesis. If the law passes this test, it is authoritative and thus functions as a second order reason which **excludes**[35] other considerations from the determination of action. In this way, the authority of law **excludes** the very considerations which might override a *prima facie* obligation to obey the law from the subject's determination of action, and thus is not properly prima facie.

However, this opposition to a *prima facie* obligation to obey the law can be addressed if we make certain changes to Raz's dependence thesis. Rather than requiring that the authority's directive reflect the reasons which apply to the subject independently, the dependence thesis should require that the authority's directive reflect those reasons for which the subject appealed to authority. In this way, the authoritative character of the directive may be undermined by those reasons which formed the basis of the obligation to obey authority. Let us look at this more closely.

The Dependence Thesis Revised

Where I think Raz went wrong, is in attempting to maintain that the authority's directive may be undermined only through its dependence on the balance of reasons it is meant to reflect. Raz does not need to maintain this in order to recognize the limitations he wishes upon authoritative directives. In fact, I will argue that it is more consistent with Raz' theory of authority (in terms of content-independent obligation) to maintain that the directive does not need to be meant to reflect the balance of reasons for action, but rather needs to reflect the reason(s) one has for appealing to authority.

In this case, the foundation of authority is again the fact that the reasons a subject has independently are more likely to be complied with if one appeals to authority, rather than acting on her own evaluation of these reasons. This justification of authority is what then serves to undermine the authority: The purposive nature of such authority provides a ground upon which the directive of the authority may be evaluated, regardless of its "content independent" imposition of obligation. If the authority's directive fails to reflect those things for which one appeals to authority, then it fails to impose an obligation to obey.

Because this second evaluation operates at a different level than the assessment of "reasons for action" which apply independently, this assessment does not threaten the "content-independent" nature of the authority's directive. The assessment which the authority's directive is meant to replace in a content-independent fashion is the assessment of "reasons for action". The assessment which serves as a "check" on authority is an assessment of reasons for assessing "reasons for action" in a particular way (namely, through appeal to authority).

Let us examine this more closely, using the model of second order reasoning within which Raz works. On the intuitive model of practical reason and action[36], one should do that which is indicated by the balance of reasons. This is a direct determination of what one's action should be. The second order reason provided by the presence of a binding authoritative directive is meant to preempt such a weighing of the balance of reasons for action, and instead appeal to the authority as the proper way to assess these reasons. However, while the second-order reason provided by the presence of a binding authoritative directive **does** preempt a weighing of the balance of reasons for action, it does **not** preempt a weighing of the balance of reasons *to take the authority's utterance as a second order reason for action.*

Whereas the balance of reasons for action inherent in the intuitive model of practical reason and action is concerned with the determination of what action one should engage in, the reasons for taking a second order reason for action are concerned with the determination of **how** one should determine the proper "balance of reasons for action". This is important, because when I discuss the "reasons for taking the authority's directive as a second order reason for action", this does not change the content-independent nature of the authority's directive. Although the content of the authority's directive **does** affect the balance of reasons for taking the directive as a second order reason for action, this is not the same as the balance of reasons the directive (if taken as a second order reason for action) is meant to replace in a content-independent fashion. The content of the directive affects only the balance of reasons for taking the authority's directive as a second order (content-independent) reason for action (the reasons to appeal to authority rather than attempting to balance the "reasons for action" oneself).

The second order reason derives its normative force from the fact that one should **not** determine (directly) what one's actions should be by weighing the balance of (first order) reasons. Rather, it indicates that one should take the authority's evaluation of the balance of reasons as content-independently binding. It also requires that, once the directive is issued, the balance of reasons continues to indicate one should take the authority's evaluation as binding. For example, we might begin with the assumption that one reason we appeal to law is to assure appropriate conduct toward others in the sense that people not be subjected to violence or torture. The laws of Nazi Germany which sought to systematically exterminate a particular race of people, then, clearly do not reflect these reasons to adopt a legal system. Likewise, laws in the deep south of the United States in the 1950s might be found to clearly violate the types of standards of conduct toward others which we adopt a legal system in order to assure. When the particular law in question violates the very reason for which the legal system was adopted in this way, it does not obligate compliance.

Let us look more closely at this example. Suppose one is a black citizen in the deep south of the United States during the 1950s. The laws of the south are such that they prohibit me from benefiting from interaction in society in the way that justified my appeal to the authority of the state in the manner of the Normal Justification Thesis. The laws of the state are meant, however, to reflect the majority opinion (or Congressional vote or whatever is required...) that they were supposed to reflect in order to qualify as authoritative under the original version of the dependence thesis (Raz's version). Since the only limitation allowed by the original dependence thesis is satisfied, one cannot override the obligation to obey the law and maintain the content-independent, second-order character of law.

On the revised dependence thesis, however, my obligation to obey is undermined by the fact that the law keeps me from benefiting from interaction in society in the manner which justified my appeal to the authority of the legal system. On the revised dependence thesis, the subject may assess the obligation to comply on the basis of the reason for adopting the law as a second order reason.

In addition, shifting the focus of the dependence thesis away from the balance of reasons which the authority's decision is meant to replace, to the reason(s) for which one appeals to authority, more consistently recognizes the content-independent nature of an authoritative directive. On Raz' version of the dependence thesis, the authority's normative force was dependent on the authority's decision being meant to reflect the balance of first-order reasons for action (the very balance of reasons it is meant to replace). On my version of the dependence thesis, the authority's normative force is dependent on the reason(s) for which one appealed to the authority. If the normative force of an authoritative directive is dependent on its being meant to reflect some balance of (first-order) reasons, the legitimate content of an authoritative directive is quite restricted. On the other hand, if the normative force of the authoritative directive is dependent on the reason(s) for which one appeals to the authority, the directive may have any content whatsoever so long as the directive does not undermine the very reason for which one appeals to authority.

Furthermore, this limitation captures what Gans refers to as "the concretization" of reasons for action. Consider the example of traffic law, and in particular the laws governing which side of the road we should drive on. We need to know which side of the road others will drive on, so we appeal to an authority's directive so that we can count on other people driving on a particular side. We do not care *why* the authority chooses a particular side of the road. We care only *that* he choose a particular side of the road. In this way, so long as he chooses one side of the road and so facilitates our driving, the reasons for appealing to authority are reflected by his directive, no matter what reasons his directive is meant to reflect.

Toward a Prima Facie Obligation to Obey the Law

Let us return now to our argument concerning the obligation to obey the law. The need for rules in a civilized society provides a presumption in favor of obedience to the law. Applying the "Normal Justification Thesis", we find that the authority of law is justified by the argument that the subject is more likely to attain the goods of civilized life if he accepts the laws of society as authoritatively binding. The obligation to obey the law, then, is established through the goods one can achieve only through society. On the revised dependence thesis, this obligation must then be subject to review by way of this basis of obligation.

Each law, then, may be assessed by the subject on the standard provided by the normal justification thesis. If the law fails to reflect the purpose for which it is adopted, it does not obligate compliance. In the above discussion, this would mean that if the law threatens the goods one achieves through interaction in society, it is not binding. It is not that this law "is not the best reason...", but rather that this law "is not justified by the idea that we're better off appealing to law..." that undermines its ability to obligate compliance. In this, those cases where "concretization" is needed are not undermined, for we would still be "better off appealing to law..." (consider the example of traffic law). But cases of laws (like racial laws) which don't reflect this justification are illegitimate.

The model of the obligation to obey the law I have presented operates on two levels. First, there is the level of establishing the obligation to obey in the manner described by the normal justification thesis. Second, there is the level of assessment which is made as to whether the law reflects the reasons I had for adopting this obligation at the first level. The first level (establishing the obligation through the normal justification thesis) operates from the perspective of the legal system as a whole. When we adopt obedience to the law as a second-order reason, we adopt this as a strategy for determining action. This means we look at reasons for adopting the second-order strategy for determining action, which is done at the level of the legal system. The second level (assessing the obligation on the basis of the reason established at the first level) operates at the level of particular laws. When we assess the law according to the reason established at the first level, we do so on a case by case basis. it is this case by case assessment of the obligation to obey the law (an obligation established at the first level) which makes the obligation prima facie.

In this way, the obligation to obey the law can be seen as both *prima facie* and general. In the manner described by the normal justification thesis, I adopt an obligation to obey the law as a second-order reason for action. However, this obligation to obey may be overridden by an evaluation that a particular law in question does not reflect the justification I had for adopting the obligation to obey the law as a second-order reason for action. In this sense it is a prima facie obligation.

Under the model of the revised dependence thesis, then, we may establish a two-level model of the obligation to obey the law which makes the authority of law limited in significant respects, and is able to retain a sense in which the law *qua* law imposes an obligation to obey. This two-level model is important, for it allows us to retain a "check" on laws passed without threatening the function of the legal system.

This "check" has two important features. First, it allows the agent to assess the obligation to obey the law in terms of the reasons which the agent has for appealing to the authority of law. In this, the obligation functions as the type of second-order reason we described in chapter five as consistent with autonomy. Thus, the model of autonomy we have explored may allow for appeal to this form of social authority.

Secondly, it retains the binding features of law *qua* law which allow the legal system to facilitate the goods we wish to attain through life in civilized society. I may not kill my companion to the movies though the balance of first-order reasons would call for it. Because I still have reason to appeal to law to gain safety from such evaluations on the part of others, the authority of laws against killing my companion still obligate compliance, and replace *this* balance of reasons for action.

Thus, the model of the authority of law I have outlined can provide the goods we wish to attain through life in a rule-governed society. In this, it enhances the autonomy of those living in that society by providing the security, stability and assurances required for the "social" projects we hold most dear. And by providing these goods through the type of obligation which is consistent with autonomy, these social enhancements of autonomy are not pitted paradoxically against a threat which social authority might pose to individual autonomy.

[1] Hayek, F.A. The Constitution of Liberty (University of Chicago Press, 1960), pp.156-157.
[2] See Raz, Joseph The Concept of a Legal System (Oxford University Press, 1970); Practical Reason and Norms (re-printed by Princeton University Press, 1990); The Authority of Law (Oxford University Press, 1979); The Morality of Freedom (Oxford University Press, 1986).
[3] Gans, Chaim Philosophical Anarchism and Political Disobedience, (New York: Cambridge University Press, 1992), p.39.
[4] See Raz, Joseph The Authority of Law, (New York: Oxford University Press, 1979), pp.234-237.
[5] See Raz, The Morality of Freedom, (New York: Oxford University Press, 1986).
[6] Raz, The Morality of Freedom, p.53.
[7] See Hart, H.L.A. Essays on Bentham (New York: Oxford University Press, 1982); Raz, Joseph Practical Reason and Norms (Princeton: Princeton University Press, 1990).
[8] Raz, The Morality of Freedom, p.42.
[9] Raz, The Authority of Law, p.237.
[10] Raz, The Authority of Law, p.238.
[11] Raz, The Authority of Law, p.238.
[12] Raz, The Authority of Law, p.238.
[13] Raz, The Authority of Law, p.238.
[14] Raz, The Authority of Law, p.239. See also Raz, "Promises and Obligation".
[15] Raz, The Authority of Law, p.239.
[16] Raz, The Authority of Law, p.239.
[17] Raz, The Authority of Law, p.239.

[18] Raz, The Authority of Law, p.239.
[19] Raz, The Authority of Law, p.240.
[20] Raz, The Authority of Law, p.240.
[21] Singer, Peter Democracy and Disobedience, (New York: Oxford University Press, 1973).
[22] Singer, Democracy and Disobedience, p.52.
[23] Raz, The Authority of Law, p.241.
[24] Singer, Democracy and Disobedience, p.38.
[25] Raz, The Authority of Law, p.242.
[26] Raz, The Authority of Law, p.242.
[27] See Raz, The Authority of Law, p.243.
[28] Raz, The Authority of Law, p.244.
[29] Raz, The Authority of Law, pp.234-237.
[30] As discussed in chapter five.
[31] Raz, The Morality of Freedom, p.41.
[32] Gans, Philosophical Anarchism and Political Disobedience, p.39.
[33] F.A. Hayek believes the predictability of the behavior of others which the law provides to be vital if people are to "control" their own lives. See The Constitution of Liberty (Chicago: University of Chicago Press, 1960), p.157; See also my paper "The Concept of Autonomy", American Philosophical Quarterly (April 1994).
[34] See H.L.A. Hart's discussion of the "rules of recognition" in The Concept of Law (New York: Oxford University Press, 1961), pp.97-107.
[35] See Raz, Practical Reason and Norms.
[36] Raz, Joseph, "Reasons for Actions, Decisions and Norms" in Raz, Joseph (ed.) Practical Reasoning, (New York: Oxford University Press, 1978), p.130.

BIBLIOGRAPHY

BIBLIOGRAPHY

Adams, Robert M. *The Virtue of Faith*. Oxford: Oxford University Press, 1987.

Aquinas, Thomas. *Summa Theologica*. in Pegis, A.C. (trans.) *Basic Writings of Saint Thomas Aquinas*. NY: Random House, 1945.

Augustine. *On Free Choice of the Will*. translated by Benjamin, Anna S. and Hackstaff, L.H. NY: Bobbs-Merrill, 1964.

Aristotle. *Ethica Eudemia*. in Barnes, Jonathan (trans.) *The Complete Works of Aristotle*. Princeton: Bollingen, 1984.

———. *Nicomachean Ethics*. in McKeon, Richard (trans.) *The Basic Works of Aristotle*. NY: Random House, 1941.

———. *Politics*. in McKeon, *The Basic Works of Aristotle*.

Austin, J.L. *Philosophical Papers*. Oxford: Clarendon Press, 1961.

———. "Three Ways of Spilling Ink." *Philosophical Review* 75 (1966): 427-40.

Austin, John. *The Province of Jurisprudence Determined* New York: Noonday Books, 1954.

Beck, Lewis White. "Apodictic Imperatives." in Wolff, Robert Paul *Kant: Foundations of the Metaphysics of Morals*.

Benn, Stanley. *A Theory of Freedom*. New York: Cambridge University Press, 1988.

Benn, Stanley and Peters, R.S. *The Principles of Political Thought*. New York: The Free Press, 1959.

Bentham, Jeremy. The Principles of Morals and Legislation. Buffalo: Prometheus Books, 1988.

Berlin, Isaiah. Four Essays on Liberty. New York: Oxford University Press, 1969.

Bond, E.J. Reason and Value. New York: Cambridge University Press, 1983.

Bryson, Lyman, Finkelstein, Louis, Maciver, R.M., and McKeon, Richard. Freedom and Authority in Our Time: Twelfth Symposium of the Conference on Science, Philosophy and Religion. New York: Kraus Reprint Co., 1971.

Cahn, Edmond N. "Authority and Responsibility." in Bryson, Lyman et.al. Freedom and Authority in Our Time New York: Kraus Reprint Co., 1971.

Child, James W. "Specific Commands, General Rules and Degrees of Autonomy." Canadian Journal of Law and Jurisprudence, vol. VIII, no.2 (July 1995).

Christman, John (ed). The Inner Citadel. New York: Oxford University Press, 1989.

Cohen, Carl. Civil Disobedience: Conscience, Tactics, and the Law. New York: Columbia University Press, 1971.

Cohen, Julius. "The Relation of Law to Freedom and Authority", in Bryson, Lyman et.al. Freedom and Authority in Our Time. New York: Kraus Reprint Co., 1971.

Cole, E.B. "'Autarkeia' in Aristotle." University of Dayton Review Vol.19, No.3 (Winter 1988-89): 35-42.

Coleman, Jules. Markets, Morals and the Law. New York: Cambridge University Press, 1988.

Dahl, Robert A. After The Revolution?: Authority in a Good Society. New Haven: Yale University Press, 1970.

Darwall, Stephen. Impartial Reason. Ithaca: Cornell University Press, 1983.

Davidson, Donald. Essays on Actions and Events. New York: Oxford University Press, 1980.

Dorsey, Gray Lankford. "The Necessity of Authority to Freedom." in Bryson, Lyman et.al. Freedom and Authority in Our Time. New York: Kraus Reprint Co., 1971.

Dworkin, Gerald. The Theory and Practice of Autonomy. New York: Cambridge University Press, 1988.

——————. "Autonomy and Behavior Control." Hastings Center Report (Feb. 1976).

Edwards, Rem B. Psychiatry and Ethics Prometheus Books, 1982.

Elster, Jon. Sour Grapes: Studies in the Subversion of Rationality. New York: Cambridge University Press, 1983.

——————. Ulysses and the Sirens: Studies in Rationality and Irrationality. New York: Cambridge University Press, 1979.

Feinberg, Joel. Harm To Self. NY: Oxford University Press, 1986.

——————. Harm to Others. NY: Oxford University Press, 1984.

——————. Rights, Justice and the Bounds of Liberty.

Princeton: Princeton University Press, 1980.

———. Social Philosophy. NJ: Prentice-Hall, 1973.

———. Doing and Deserving. Princeton: Princeton University Press, 1970.

Fingarette, Herbert. Heavy Drinking. Berkeley: University of California Press, 1988.

———. The Meaning of Criminal Insanity. Berkeley: University of California Press, 1972.

Finnis, John. Natural Law and Natural Rights. New York: Oxford University Press, 1980.

Fischer, John Martin (ed.). Moral Responsibility. Ithaca: Cornell University Press, 1986.

Flew, Antony. A Rational Animal. Oxford University Press, 1978.

———. David Hume: Philosopher of Moral Science. Oxford: Basil Blackwell, 1986.

Flew, Antony and Vesey, Godfrey. Agency and Necessity. Oxford: Basil Blackwell, 1987.

Frankfurt, Harry. "Freedom of the Will and the Concept of a Person." Journal of Philosophy 68 (Jan. 1971): 5-20.

———. "Alternate Possibilities and Moral Responsibility." Journal of Philosophy 66 (Dec. 1969): 828-39.

Frey, R.G. "Moral standing, The Value of Lives, and Speciesism." Unpublished Paper.

———. "Butler on Self-Love and Benevolence." Unpublished Paper.

———. "The Significance of Agency and Marginal Cases." Philosophica 39, (1987): 39-46.

———. "Autonomy and the Value of Animal Life." The Monist Vol.70, no.1 (Jan.1987): 50-63.

———. "Autonomy and Conceptions of the Good Life." in Sumner, L.W., Attig, Thomas and Callen, Donald (eds.) Values and Moral Standing (Bowling Green Studies in Applied Philosophy, 1986).

Frey, R.G. and Morris, Christopher. Law and Liability. New York: Cambridge University Press, 1991.

———. Value, Welfare and Morality. New York: Cambridge University Press, 1993.

Friedman, R.B. "On the Concept of Authority in Political Philosophy." in Raz, Joseph (ed.) Authority 1990.

Friedrich, Carl (ed.). Nomos I: Authority. Cambridge: Harvard University Press, 1958.

———. "Authority, Reason and Discretion." in Friedrich, Carl (ed.) Nomos I: Authority 1958.

Fuller, Lon. The Morality of Law. Yale University Press, 1964.

Gans, Chaim. Philosophical Anarchism and Political Disobedience. New York: Cambridge University Press, 1992.

Gray, John. Mill on Liberty: A Defence. Boston: Routledge and

Kegan Paul, 1983.

———. Liberalism. University of Minnesota Press, 1986.

———. Hayek On Liberty. New York: Basil Blackwell, 1984.

Griffin, James. Well-Being. Oxford University Press, 1986.

Green, Leslie. The Authority of the State. Oxford University Press, 1988.

Green, Ronald M. "Abraham, Isaac and the Jewish Tradition: An Ethical Reappraisal." The Journal of Religious Ethics Vol.10, No.1, (Spring 1982).

Green, T.H. Lectures on the Principles of Political Obligation. ed. by Harris, Paul and Morrow, John New York: Cambridge University Press, 1986.

Greenawalt, Kent. Conflicts of Law and Morality. New York: Oxford University Press, 1989.

Griffiths, A. Phillips (ed.). Of Liberty. New York: Cambridge University Press, 1983.

Hall, Jerome. "Authority and the Law." in Friedrich, Carl (ed.) Nomos I: Authority 1958.

Hare, R.M. Freedom and Reason. Oxford University Press, 1963.

Hart, H.L.A. Essays on Bentham. Oxford, Clarendon Press, 1982.

———. Punishment and Responsibility. Oxford University Press, 1968.

———. The Concept of Law. Oxford University Press, 1961.

Hart, H.L.A. and Honore, Tony. Causation in the Law Oxford University Press, 1959.

Haworth, Lawrence. Autonomy. Yale University Press, 1986.

Hayek, F.A. The Constitution of Liberty. University of Chicago Press, 1960.

Hendel, Charles. "An Exploration of the Nature of Authority." in Friedrich, Carl (ed.) Nomos I: Authority 1958.

Herzog, Don. Happy Slaves. University of Chicago Press, 1989.

Hill, Thomas. Autonomy and Self-Respect. (Cambridge University Press, 1991.

———. Dignity and Practical Reason. Cornell University Press, 1992.

Hobbes, Thomas. Leviathan. ed. by Oakeshott, Michael New York: Collier Books/Macmillian Publishing Co., 1962.

Kant, Immanuel. Grounding for the Metaphysics of Morals. Translated by James W. Ellington, Indianapolis: Hackett Publishing Co., 1981.

Katz, Leo. Bad Acts and Guilty Minds. Chicago University Press, 1986.

Kenny, Anthony. Freewill and Responsibility. London: Routledge, 1978.

———. The Metaphysics of Mind. Oxford: Clarendon Press, 1989.

Keyt, David, and Miller, Fred D. (eds.). <u>A Companion to Aristotle's Politics</u>. New York: Basil Blackwell, 1991.

Knight, Frank H. "Authority and the Free Society." in Friedrich, Carl (ed.) <u>Nomos I: Authority</u> 1958.

Kupfer, Joseph. <u>Autonomy and Social Interaction</u>. Albany: State University of New York Press, 1990.

Leigh, L.H. <u>Strict and Vicarious Liability</u>. London: Sweet and Maxwell, 1982.

Lomasky, Loren. <u>Persons, Rights, and the Moral Community</u>. Oxford University Press, 1987.

⎯⎯⎯⎯. "Liberal Autonomy." <u>Philosophy and Theology,</u> (1990): 297-309.

Macken, John S.J. <u>The Autonomy Theme in the Church Dogmatics</u>. Cambridge University Press, 1990.

May, Thomas. "The Concept of Autonomy." <u>American Philosophical Quarterly</u> (April 1994).

⎯⎯⎯⎯. "The Nurse Under Physician Authority." <u>Journal of Medical Ethics</u> (Dec. 1993).

Mele, Alfred. <u>Irrationality</u>. Oxford University Press, 1987.

Milligan, David. <u>Reasoning and the Explanation of Actions</u>. NJ: Humanities Press, 1980.

Molnar, Thomas. <u>Authority and Its Enemies</u>. NY: Arlington House Publishers, 1976.

Moore, Michael S. "Authority, Law, and Razian Reasons." Southern California Law Review, vol.62, nos.3&4 (March-May 1989).

———. Law and Psychiatry. Cambridge University Press, 1984.

Morigiwa, Yasutomo. "Authority, Rationality, and Law: Joseph Raz and the Practice of Law." Southern California Law Review, Vol.62, nos.3&4 (March-May 1989).

Nagel, Thomas. Mortal Questions. Cambridge University Press, 1979.

———. The Possibility of Altruism. Princeton University Press, 1970.

Negley, Glenn. "Legal Imperative and Moral Authority." in Bryson, Lyman et.al. Freedom and Authority in Our Time New York: Kraus Reprint Co., 1971.

Nozick, Robert. Anarchy, State and Utopia. New York: Basic Books, 1974.

O'Neil, Onora. Constructions of Reason. Cambridge University Press, 1989.

O'Neil (Nell), Onora. Acting On Principle. Columbia University Press, 1975.

Patterson, Edwin W. "Freedom and Legal Authority: The Kinds of Authority of Law." in Bryson, Lyman et.al. Freedom and Authority in Our Time New York: Kraus Reprint Co., 1971.

Parfit, Derek. Reasons and Persons. Oxford University Press, 1984.

Perry, Stephen. "Second-Order Reasons, Uncertainty and Legal Theory." <u>Southern California Law Review</u>, Vol.62, nos.3&4, (March-May 1989).

Pettit, Philip. "Humeans, Anti-Humeans, and Motivation." <u>Mind</u> (1987).

Rawls, John. <u>A Theory of Justice</u>. Harvard University Press, 1971.

——————— "Two Concepts of Rules." <u>Philosophical Review</u>, Vol.64 (1955).

Raz, Joseph. <u>Practical Reason and Norms</u>. Princeton University Press, 1990.

———————. <u>Authority</u>. Albany: State University of New York Press, 1990.

———————. "Facing Up: A Reply." <u>Southern California Law Review</u> Vol.62, nos.3&4 (March-May 1989).

———————. <u>The Morality of Freedom</u>. Oxford University Press, 1986.

———————. <u>The Authority of Law</u>. Oxford University Press, 1979.

———————. <u>Practical Reasoning</u>. Oxford University Press, 1978.

———————. <u>The Concept of a Legal System</u>. Oxford University Press, 1970.

———————. "Authority and Consent." <u>Virginia Law Review</u> Vol.67.

Regan, Donald H. "Authority and Value: Reflections on Raz's Morality of Freedom." Southern California Law Review Vol.62, nos.3&4 (March-May 1989).

Richards, David A.J. Sex, Drugs, Death and the Law. Rowman and Littlefield, 1982.

——————. A Theory of Reasons for Action. Oxford: Clarendon Press, 1971.

Robins, Michael. Promising, Intending and Moral Autonomy. Cambridge University Press, 1984.

Robinson, Daniel N. Psychology and Law. Oxford University Press, 1980.

Rorty, A.E. Mind in Action. Boston: Beacon Press, 1988.

——————. The Identities of Persons. University of California Press, 1976.

Rosenbaum, Max (ed.). Compliant Behavior: Beyond Obedience to Authority. NY: Human Sciences Press, 1983.

Sartorius, Rolf (ed.). Paternalism. University of Minnesota Press, 1983.

—————— Individual Conduct and Social Norms. Belmont: Dickenson Publishing Company, 1975.

Schelling, Thomas C. Micromotives and Macrobehavior. New York: W.W. Norton & Co., 1978.

Sher, George. Desert. Princeton University Press, 1987.

Shiner, Roger. "Exclusionary and Expressive Reasons."
Unpublished paper.

──────. "Law and Authority." <u>Canadian Journal of Law and Jurisprudence</u>, Vol.2, no.1 (Jan.1989): 3-18.

Shoeman, Ferdinand. <u>Responsibility, Character and the Emotions</u>. Cambridge University Press, 1987.

Simmons, A. John. <u>Moral Principles and Political Obligations</u>. Princeton University Press, 1979.

Simpson, A.W. Brian. <u>Cannibalism and the Common Law</u>. University of Chicago Press, 1984.

Simon, Yves. <u>A General Theory of Authority</u>. University of Notre Dame Press, 1962.

Smith, Michael. "The Humean Theory of Motivation." <u>Mind</u> (1987): 36-61.

──────. "On Humeans, Anti-Humeans, and Motivation: A Reply to Pettit." <u>Mind</u> (Oct.1988): 589-595.

Spiro, Herbert J. "Authority, Values and Policy." in Friedrich, Carl (ed.) <u>Nomos I: Authority</u> 1958.

Sorabji, Richard. <u>Necessity, Cause, and Blame</u>. Cornell University Press, 1980.

Strawson, P.F. "Freedom and Resentment." <u>Proceedings of the British Academy</u> 48.

Szasz, Thomas. <u>Law, Liberty and Psychiatry</u>. New York: Macmillan, 1963.

BIBLIOGRAPHY

Taylor, Charles. "Responsibility for Self." in Rorty, A.E. The Identities of Persons 1976.

Taylor, Telford. Nuremberg and Vietnam: An American Tragedy. New York: Bantam Books, 1971.

Thomson, Judith Jarvis. Acts and Other Events. Cornell University Press, 1977.

Waldron, Jeremy. "Autonomy and Perfectionism in Raz's Morality of Freedom." Southern California Law Review Vol.62, nos.3&4 (March-May 1989).

Watson, Gary. "Free Agency." Journal of Philosophy 72 (April 1975): 205-20.

Wertheimer, Alan. Coercion Princeton University Press, 1987.

White, Alan R. Grounds of Liability. Oxford University Press, 1985.

Wilkerson, T.E. "Desire, Belief and Rational Action." Ratio XXVIII (Dec. 1986).

Wolf, Susan. Freedom Within Reason. Oxford University Press, 1990.

——————— "Sanity and the Metaphysics of Responsibility." in Shoeman, Ferdinand Responsibility, Character and the Emotions 1987.

Wolff, Robert Paul. In Defense of Anarchism New York: Harper and Row Publishers, 1970.

———————. Kant: Foundations of the Metaphysics of Morals: (Text and Critical Essays). New York: Bobbs-Merrill, 1969.

Wright, Georg Henrik Von. <u>Norm and Action</u>. London: Routledge and Kegan Paul, 1963.

Williams, Bernard. <u>Moral Luck</u>. Cambridge University Press, 1981.

Young, Robert. <u>Personal Autonomy</u>. NY: St. Martin's Press, 1986.

Law and Philosophy Library

1. E. Bulygin, J.-L. Gardies and I. Niiniluoto (eds.): *Man, Law and Modern Forms of Life.* With an Introduction by M.D. Bayles. 1985 ISBN 90-277-1869-5
2. W. Sadurski: *Giving Desert Its Due.* Social Justice and Legal Theory. 1985
   ISBN 90-277-1941-1
3. N. MacCormick and O. Weinberger: *An Institutional Theory of Law.* New Approaches to Legal Positivism. 1986 ISBN 90-277-2079-7
4. A. Aarnio: *The Rational as Reasonable.* A Treatise on Legal Justification. 1987
   ISBN 90-277-2276-5
5. M.D. Bayles: *Principles of Law.* A Normative Analysis. 1987
   ISBN 90-277-2412-1; Pb: 90-277-2413-X
6. A. Soeteman: *Logic in Law.* Remarks on Logic and Rationality in Normative Reasoning, Especially in Law. 1989 ISBN 0-7923-0042-4
7. C.T. Sistare: *Responsibility and Criminal Liability.* 1989 ISBN 0-7923-0396-2
8. A. Peczenik: *On Law and Reason.* 1989 ISBN 0-7923-0444-6
9. W. Sadurski: *Moral Pluralism and Legal Neutrality.* 1990 ISBN 0-7923-0565-5
10. M.D. Bayles: *Procedural Justice.* Allocating to Individuals. 1990 ISBN 0-7923-0567-1
11. P. Nerhot (ed.): *Law, Interpretation and Reality.* Essays in Epistemology, Hermeneutics and Jurisprudence. 1990 ISBN 0-7923-0593-0
12. A.W. Norrie: *Law, Ideology and Punishment.* Retrieval and Critique of the Liberal Ideal of Criminal Justice. 1991 ISBN 0-7923-1013-6
13. P. Nerhot (ed.): *Legal Knowledge and Analogy.* Fragments of Legal Epistemology, Hermeneutics and Linguistics. 1991 ISBN 0-7923-1065-9
14. O. Weinberger: *Law, Institution and Legal Politics.* Fundamental Problems of Legal Theory and Social Philosophy. 1991 ISBN 0-7923-1143-4
15. J. Wróblewski: *The Judicial Application of Law.* Edited by Z. Bańkowski and N. MacCormick. 1992 ISBN 0-7923-1569-3
16. T. Wilhelmsson: *Critical Studies in Private Law.* A Treatise on Need-Rational Principles in Modern Law. 1992 ISBN 0-7923-1659-2
17. M.D. Bayles: *Hart's Legal Philosophy.* An Examination. 1992 ISBN 0-7923-1981-8
18. D.W.P. Ruiter: *Institutional Legal Facts.* Legal Powers and their Effects. 1993
    ISBN 0-7923-2441-2
19. J. Schonsheck: *On Criminalization.* An Essay in the Philosophy of the Criminal Law. 1994
    ISBN 0-7923-2663-6
20. R.P. Malloy and J. Evensky (eds.): *Adam Smith and the Philosophy of Law and Economics.* 1994 ISBN 0-7923-2796-9
21. Z. Bankowski, I. White and U. Hahn (eds.): *Informatics and the Foundations of Legal Reasoning.* 1995 ISBN 0-7923-3455-8
22. E. Lagerspetz: *The Opposite Mirrors.* An Essay on the Conventionalist Theory of Institutions. 1995 ISBN 0-7923-3325-X
23. M. van Hees: *Rights and Decisions.* Formal Models of Law and Liberalism. 1995
    ISBN 0-7923-3754-9
24. B. Anderson: *"Discovery" in Legal Decision-Making.* 1996 ISBN 0-7923-3981-9

GENERAL THEOLOGICAL SEMINARY
NEW YORK

DATE DUE

APR 1 9 1999			

Printed in USA

HIGHSMITH #45230